The Welfare Marketplace

CENTER
for **PUBLIC**
SERVICE

The Brookings Institution established the Center for Public Service in 1999 to improve the odds that America's most talented citizens will choose careers in the public service. Toward that goal, the center is committed to rigorous research and practical recommendations for making public service more attractive, be it in traditional government settings, nonprofit agencies, or the growing number of private firms that provide services once delivered inside government. As the center's logo suggests, the single-sectored, government-centered public service of the 1970s has been replaced by the multisectored, highly mobile public service of today. The center was created to track the rise of this new public service, while making sure that both government and the nonprofit sector can compete for their fair share of talent in an ever-tightening labor market.

As part of this effort, the Center for Public Service is committed to publishing timely reports on the state of the public service. These reports, which vary in length from short reports to books, attempt to lay the foundation for long-needed policy reforms. Because these reports are designed to move quickly into publication, some will not be verified to the same level of detail as other Brookings publications. As with all Brookings publications, the judgments, conclusions, and recommendations presented in any individual study are solely those of the author or authors and should not be attributed to the trustees, officers, or other staff members of the institution.

M. BRYNA SANGER

The Welfare Marketplace

PRIVATIZATION AND WELFARE REFORM

BROOKINGS INSTITUTION PRESS
Washington, D.C.

Library of Congress Cataloging-in-Publication data

Sanger, Mary Bryna.
    The welfare marketplace : privatization and welfare reform / M. Bryna Sanger.
        p.   cm.
    Includes bibliographical references.
    ISBN 0-8157-7705-1 (paper : alk. paper)
    1. Public welfare—Contracting out—United States.   2. Welfare recipients—Employment—United States.   I. Title.

HV91 .S253 2003
361.6'8'0973—dc21   2003007090

9 8 7 6 5 4 3 2 1

The paper used in this publication meets minimum requirements of the American National Standard for Information Sciences—Permanence of Paper for Printed Library Materials: ANSI Z39.48-1992.

Typeset in Sabon

Composition by Betsy Kulamer
Washington, D.C.

Printed by R. R. Donnelley
Harrisonburg, Virginia

Contents

Foreword

The phrase "reinventing government" has been in and out of fashion in recent years, and it has been controversial even when fashionable. Nonetheless, those two words capture an original and enduring impulse of the American political system: government is a work in progress. It can always be improved—part of the process and purpose of government is its own reinvention.

That idea is also at the core of the Brookings Institution's research agenda. Our founder, Robert S. Brookings, came to Washington at the beginning of the last century to help the Wilson administration make government more efficient, and he stayed on in the nation's capital to advance that goal by setting up the prototypical think tank, the forerunner of this institution.

Therefore this report by Byrna Sanger for our Center on Public Service is a quintessential Brookings publication. She looks back over the past two decades, when the repurcussions of the Reagan revolution, with its emphasis on paring back "big government," have meant that government at all levels has had to do more with less. Reinventing government has entailed a reassessment of its role in financing, producing, and delivering public services. While there has been a global movement in public management that has demanded smaller, cheaper, and more effective government, in the United States the public management revolution has followed its own course, consistent with its particular history and values and with popular distrust of government. The efforts epitomized by the Clinton-era National Performance Review emphasized efforts that worked better and cost less and a reconsideration of what government ought to do. Increasingly, this has meant that authority has been devolved from the federal government to the states, and the means and character of public service reform have varied around the country. Nevertheless, contracting out and increasing reliance on private markets have characterized the movement nationwide.

Welfare reform came in 1996 with the passage of the Personal Responsibility and Work Opportunity Reconciliation Act, just in time to ride the crest of this reform movement. It challenged states and localities to develop new delivery systems and services to move welfare recipients from welfare to work. Examination of its design and implementation around the country reveals considerable variation in how jurisdictions have responded. The design of delivery systems, the number and character of providers selected, and the terms under which they work differ, but a few patterns are evident: local governments depend more on contractors to provide services, and increasingly these are private for-profit firms. The law's emphasis on engaging large proportions of welfare caseloads in employment-related activities and the strict federal deadlines for required job placement of welfare recipients under the Temporary Assistance for Needy Families (TANF) program have tested local capacities everywhere. The result has been that forty-nine states and the District of Columbia now do some contracting at either the state or local levels, and 27 percent of all state contracts have been with private for-profit providers. In some states and localities the proportion is much higher. Government agencies had historically provided welfare services in some states and localities; in many others, nonprofits played a dominant role. Increasingly government agencies and nonprofit providers now compete with for-profit firms in the same market.

Bryna, a professor of urban policy at the New School who has consulted widely for state and local governments, explores the implications of the increasing privatization of welfare-to-work services, and especially the competition with public and nonprofit providers that welfare reform has spawned. (The preliminary findings of this study were presented at a Brookings forum titled "A View from the Frontlines: Innovations in the Delivery of Welfare Services" in October 2001.) Her close examination of four jurisdictions—New York City, Milwaukee, San Diego, and Houston—reveals the challenges to governance and the health of a multisectored economy that arise when market rules govern public provision, especially for vulnerable populations. When the private sector competes and market incentives dominate, the boundaries between the sectors blur, creating some desirable improvements in public management but at the same time possibly compromising the historic missions of nonprofits.

When market imperatives clash with social missions, the battlefield is strewn with casualties. Public and nonprofit providers are at risk of losing their capacity and sometimes their souls. Other organizations, unwilling or unable to adjust to the new market rules, are simply disappearing. Thus this report is a cautionary tale, taking the developments in welfare to work as a case study of the difficult choices and serious limitations posed by the use of markets for human services. Responsible public authorities must play a greater regulatory role in this new complex of providers. Improving public performance by harnessing the virtues of the market will require more, not less, government management and oversight. Public agencies need capacity to select competent and responsible providers, to manage them and ensure accountability, and to design contract systems to reward them without creating perverse incentives or distortions in their disposition to serve the public interest. These developments are relatively recent; contracting and competition show promise—but the risks are great. Government's reliance on the private sector may have grown faster than its ability to manage it. This book, we hope, will help close that gap.

STROBE TALBOTT
President

Washington, D.C.
April 2003

Acknowledgments

The Center for Public Service at Brookings, its able staff, its visionary leader, Paul Light, and the generous funding of the Ford Foundation were instrumental in encouraging and supporting the research for this book. Paul is always ahead of the curve in understanding subtle changes in institutional and behavioral dynamics that are exerting significant influence on the future of public service. His work on the changing nature of the public service (*The New Public Service*, Brookings 1999) was instrumental in shaping the focus of this project.

Significant field work and research at a time when policy and program change did not stop for a researcher's convenience necessitated continual updating of data and vigilance in monitoring changing arrangements. Three exceedingly able research assistants helped manage the ongoing data flow from state and local governments under study and the changing arrangements and behavior of their private and nonprofit contractors. Philippe Rosse, a senior research assistant at Brookings, did much of the foundational research on each jurisdiction's contracting system and each contractor's history. He also did much of the initial interviewing of contractors and public officials in Houston. He was an enthusiastic and tireless booster for the project in the early stages, when the value of our efforts was not yet entirely clear. Cathy Leather took over ably when Philippe left Brookings to try his own hand at nonprofit management. A student in the nonprofit management program at the New School University's Robert J. Milano School of Management and Urban Policy, Cathy was a consummate professional, inducing recalcitrant bureaucrats to part with their data and successfully managing the field trips that were so important to the research. Finally, Wendy Trull saw the project to completion, still checking budget allocations, policy changes, and contractors' behavior long after her graduation and sometimes at night while holding down a new day job at New York City's Office of Management and Budget. The devil was in the details, and my able research assistants were masters at wrestling with them.

The New School University's provost, Elizabeth Dickey, and the Milano Graduate School's dean, Edward Blakley, were especially supportive of the work and its completion, granting me a sabbatical at an important time. Much of the early work was previewed at faculty seminars at Milano, and valuable feedback from a very engaged faculty made the work better. I also had the good fortune to work with the Brookings Welfare Reform and Beyond project, which in October 2001 cosponsored a Brookings forum on our preliminary findings, also published by the Center for Public Service as a Reform Watch policy brief, "When the Private Sector Competes." Excellent feedback from Ruth McCambridge and others at the Nonprofit Quarterly sharpened many ideas. Wise colleagues at the Association for Public Policy Analysis and Management's Annual Reseach Conference provided a stimulating forum to debate and scrutinize early findings and ultimate conclusions of the research in conference sessions over three years. Robert Behn, Ellen Schall, and Karen Paget were particularly helpful in shaping my thinking, and Edwin Melendez and Rikki Abzug at the New School provided critical and alternative perspectives that altered my interpretations. To all of them, I am grateful.

Finally, the able and professional staff at the Brookings Institution Press made the publication process easy. Deborah Styles's careful and sensitive editing and Janet Walker's management of the editorial process improved the product immeasurably. Becky Clark's keen marketing sense was just what was required. For all remaining errors and omissions, I accept responsibility.

*The Welfare
Marketplace*

CHAPTER ONE

Public Services and Blurring Sectoral Boundaries: An Introduction

Sectoral boundaries are blurring as governments at every level rely more and more on private markets to deliver services. The reasons for this shift are as much political as economic. The shift toward privatization is generally explained with economic arguments that stress costs and benefits, efficiency, and program management. However, public officials' current romance with the market "is really a watershed about governance, the uses of power in society, and the boundaries between public action and private concerns."[1]

Some local public services financed by states and localities have long been contracted out to private providers. Building of roads and construction of schools are examples. Other services like child welfare, home health care, and youth services have been provided by both nonprofit and for-profit providers. Others, such as prisons and fire services, are only rarely provided by a nongovernmental unit of any kind.[2] However, no public service function seems immune to privatization. The current environment reflects an increasing interest in market solutions that has encouraged outsourcing and competition, even in areas rarely considered before. In order to reflect on the size and direction of shifts in the provision of services and also to examine the trends and possible consequences of these shifts, this study limits itself to welfare-to-work services—a service area only recently experiencing change as a result of the mandates of new federal welfare reform legislation. This focus will establish a baseline from which to compare alternative arrangements for service delivery.

Devolution and Welfare Reform

Devolution, both from the federal government to the states and from the states to county and local governments, provides a unique opportunity to observe sectoral changes in delivery of public services. Most states and localities have been seizing the opportunities provided by a loosening of federal mandates, responsibilities, and authority to restructure the arrangements for provision of services.[3] Nowhere have the changes in organizational arrangements been more dramatic than in the welfare reform and work force development systems, where they were catalyzed by the Personal Responsibility and Work Opportunity Reconciliation Act (PRWORA) of 1996, the welfare reform act.[4] As a consequence of this legislation the new Temporary Assistance to Needy Families program (TANF) requires states to move increasing percentages of their welfare caseloads from public assistance to employment. States were to have placed 25 percent of their welfare clients in work by 1997 and 50 percent by 2002, or they would risk losing federal funding.[5] This has increased states' investment in job readiness, work experience, and direct job placement activities. TANF also eased federal restrictions on the use of for-profits, allowing local governments increasingly to expand the role of the private sector in meeting their needs in technology, systems management, training, and placement.[6] Around the country provision of services is being restructured, with case management, assessment, referral, job readiness, and placement organized and provided in new ways.

Many jurisdictions have long used local nonprofits—community-based organizations (CBOs) among them—to provide job training, job readiness, and placement activities under U.S. Department of Labor (DOL) programs funded by the Job Training Partnership Act (JTPA). Now, however, there is a dramatic increase in the use of private contractors—especially a few large organizations with experience in human services.[7] These large national for-profit corporations are playing increasingly dominant roles, and the effects of their participation are not yet well understood.

Goals of the Research

This report is intended to shape the discourse about the blurring of sectoral boundaries and the changing role of government and to identify the forces driving the particular shape and response of public and private organizations to these pressures to compete. I set out to assess the changes in the ways states and localities contracted out the provision of public services and to evaluate the potential impact of these trends on services, citizens, and governance. Since competition among the sectors may be inducing changes in the structure and behavior of public, private, and nonprofit organizations, my research also investigated potential shifts in the missions, management, strategy, and capacity of competing institutions. These changes may affect the success of individual organizations in this environment, but they are also likely to affect the capacity of a multisectored service sector to meet a set of highly diverse needs of a modern urban society.

I undertook a "reconnaissance mission" in the form of a series of case studies in a single service area. Welfare reform challenged states to redesign delivery systems to move large number of clients from welfare to work quickly. While this analysis relies principally on four sites contracting for welfare-to-work services, the observations may have relevance in other jurisdictions and service areas. The insights gleaned from the study of a single service area in strategically selected sites should strengthen a set of hypotheses about how these contracting efforts are likely to alter the role and capacity of each sector to provide public services. A larger national survey would be necessary to determine with certainty the effects across many different service areas, and none has been conducted to date.[8] Even so, some interesting hypotheses are beginning to emerge, painting a picture of shifting sectoral relationships and an altered environment for public and nonprofit agencies.

The chapters that follow address four major questions. First, how significant is contracting out as a form of providing public services? Second, what are the major ambitions of state and local governments when they outsource their welfare-to-work efforts, and how have they designed their delivery systems to meet their objectives? Third, how have both the nonprofits and the for-profits been meeting the challenges around the country? Fourth, what are the risks and challenges when the private sector competes in these markets?

Designing the "Reconnaissance Mission": Methodology

I was particularly interested in investigating the effects when private for-profit contractors were part of the mix in an implicitly competitive service sector. In the jurisdictions chosen for the study, the organization of service delivery to welfare clients is undergoing significant restructuring, and the number and character of contractors for serving TANF clients have changed. These jurisdictions have introduced innovations in the provision of services, particularly competition among vendors from each of the sectors, and are working with new kinds of contracting arrangements—especially for selecting and remunerating contractors. My goal was to begin to assess the motivation, strategy, and potential effects of the introduction of market forces on organizations, clients, and governance.[9]

Four jurisdictions met the criteria: San Diego, Milwaukee, New York City, and Houston (see box 1-1).[10] They represented different models of service delivery, but all included a mix of providers. Interviews were conducted in each site with current contractors (public, private, and nonprofit), public officials with significant responsibility for the design and management of the new systems, a selection of subcontractors or previous contractors who had lost out in the most recent contracting period, opinion leaders, and some researchers studying aspects of the transitions. Public documents, including contracts, newspapers, requests for proposals (RFPs), company websites, and published reports, were reviewed. Since each jurisdiction is in a different stage of implementation—some completing their second round of contracts and others still in the first round—sites could not be compared on the basis of performance. The findings below, therefore, do not speak to the ultimate effects of these arrangements on the jurisdictions' success in reducing costs, improving efficiency, or enhancing the long-term well-being of their clients, but instead suggest their likelihood of doing so and identify researchable questions about likely consequences.

Presumably, the traditional motivation, behavior, and practices of for-profits, nonprofits, and public agencies would change as a result of competition and market pressures. Indeed, the study showed that there is more variation in organizations *within* the sectors than *between* them. Size and experience matter. A large nonprofit like Goodwill in New York looks more like some of its private-sector competitors than some of the smaller CBOs.

Market forces appear to be simultaneously inducing favorable creative adaptations among some innovative nonprofits even as they have threatened the viability of others. Further, increased contracting, especially to large organizations, changes the role and capacity of government, threatening accountability and responsiveness to groups with special needs even as it relieves local government of other roles it has traditionally performed poorly. Thus I was interested in how government agencies have adapted to their altered roles.

When the Private Sector Competes

This book reports the findings of interviews with major players and observers of these changes in the provision of welfare services. The interviews showed how competitive contracting arrangements have changed the ways vendors and government agencies serve their clients. Changing the roles and behaviors of providers from all three sectors influences the character and quality of governance and therefore warrants close monitoring. This reconnaissance mission is not the last word on these issues, but these initial observations may identify the areas where public officials, policy analysts, and advocates need to maintain considerable vigilance.

The observations from my reconnaissance reported in the following chapters support several conclusions. The competitive contracting environment has had mixed results. Some of the market incentives have worked in the expected direction: in a number of nonprofits increasing innovation has improved the organization and performance of their services. At the same time, both for-profits and nonprofits are quickly draining talent and capacity as they compete for experienced executives from government and from one another. Substantial resources are necessary for local governments to be smart buyers and good contract managers. Adequate accountability and contract monitoring functions require far greater human capital and expenditures than are typically expected or budgeted for. Valuable and worthy nonprofits are becoming more businesslike; some have even formed for-profit subsidiaries. However, they also shows signs of "losing their souls" in their capitulation to market imperatives. Still others risk extinction. Contracting out and the competitive environment it spawns are clearly no panacea. New delivery approaches bring new challenges. For all the improvements in performance that they promise, they raise troubling questions about quality and accountability. The trends are unlikely to reverse themselves, but studying the problems can help design a midcourse correction.

The lessons in this study are meant to sound a warning and to induce a productive response. Scholars and practitioners need to develop a

Box 1-1. *Overview of Contract Characteristics in Four Cities*

Houston

TANF client placement: Clients are assigned to one of 30 career centers by zip code.

Providers and sites per provider: Six contractors each with multiple career centers.

Services provided to TANF clients: Centers are assigned TANF clients; receive case management services including assessment, employment planning, job readiness and job search; refer clients for intensive job and basic skills training and on-the-job training.

Bidding process: Request for proposal.

Contract structure and measurement parameters: Cost reimbursement: Each contractor must achieve certain levels for eligible served, clients receiving continued service, clients entering employment, and clients employed above minimum wage.

Level of subcontracting: Relatively little.

Milwaukee

TANF client placement: TANF clients are assigned to one of six geographic regions, each with a sole provider.

Providers and sites per provider: Five contractors, all serving a single region except one that has received two regions.

Services provided to TANF clients: Contractors complete eligibility determination and provide complete services all the way through job training and placement.

Bidding process: Request for proposal.

Contract structure and measurement parameters: Pay for performance: Contractor must achieve and can receive bonuses for achieving an entered-employment placement rate, average wage rate, job retention rate, available health insurance benefits, full and proper engagement, and basic education/job skills activities; two optional measurements (faith-based contracts and basic education/job skills attainment) may be substituted for the bonus portion of two of the above categories.

Level of subcontracting: Extensive.

New York

TANF client placement: TANF contracts are referred by Human Resources Administration (HRA) first to a Skills Assessment and Job Placement Center (SAP) contractor. If still without employment HRA will refer client to an Employment Services and Job Placement Center (ESP) contractor.

Providers and sites per provider: Five contractors with the SAP contracts; 12 contractors with the ESP contracts.

Services provided to TANF clients: SAP contractors receive TANF clients and provide skills assessments and services through preliminary job placement centers.

ESP contractors are referred clients who are not placed by the SAP contractors; they offer more intensive employment services and job training and placement.

Bidding process: Negotiated acquisition process.

Contract structure and measurement parameters: Pay for performance: SAP—payment is given for assessment, engagement in employment activities, job placement (higher rate for 30+ hours), with a bonus given for "high" wages and 90-day placement.

ESP—A percentage of base rate or a flat fee is paid for placement and 90-day retention, while a higher flat fee is paid for "high wages," left welfare, or placement for 180 days.

Level of subcontracting: Very little for SAP; extensive for ESP.

San Diego

TANF client placement: TANF clients are assigned to one of six geographic regions, each with a sole provider.

Providers and sites per provider: Two contractors run single regions, while both county officials and Lockheed Martin each run two regions.

Services provided to TANF clients: Centers are assigned clients; they handle all case-management duties including appraisal, assessment, and job search training; if clients do not succeed in finding employment, they are referred to a work placement network.

Bidding process: Request for proposal.

Contract structure and measurement parameters: Pay for performance: Certain amounts are paid for participant engagement, active caseload, 30-day employment, and 180-day employment.

Level of subcontracting: Very little.

more nuanced and sophisticated set of expectations about the costs and benefits of increased market arrangements for service delivery. Harnessing the virtues of the market will require more, not less, government management and oversight. Government's reliance on the private sector may have grown faster than its ability to manage it.[11] Difficult trade-offs are inevitable.

The study's findings should also serve as a warning to nonprofits whose future is increasingly tied to government contracts. High-performing, mission-driven organizations will have to change to remain relevant. New and blurring boundaries require new capacities, more innovation, and new kinds of collaborative relationships. The seductiveness of large government contracts and a desire to make a difference in a reengineered human services industry must be tempered by a balanced assessment of mission and capacities. Nonprofits differ among themselves as much as or more than they differ from their for-profit competitors. Each type brings different capacities, experiences, and comparative advantages. A commercialized service environment places new demands on all participants and, indeed, changes the likely success of many. Nonprofits have held a unique place in the civic infrastructure. This study thus pays particular attention to the effects of the changing environment on these critical social institutions.

The next chapter begins by placing the recent developments in context, first by reviewing the principal concerns that drove this study and then by describing the classic privatization debate that represents the foundation on which most rationales for government contracting rest. Reviewing what existing survey data show about the extent of contracting in subnational jurisdictions establishes the scale of recent changes. Chapter three explores the motivations of each of the study's jurisdictions for restructuring its delivery system, the nature of the changes made, and their expectations for performance. Chapters four and five explore the experiences of nonprofits and for-profits as they answer the call to do government's business under welfare reform. Chapter six offers some reflections about what the reconnaissance revealed and suggests some caveats about the future.

CHAPTER TWO

Contracting and Competition: The Changing Shape of Government

A welfare recipient walking into a one-stop employment center to seek job search assistance, required
under the conditions of her grant, may be greeted by a case manager
employed by a large private company like MAXIMUS or a nonprofit
employment services firm like Goodwill Industries. The company's name
and logo might be on the door, or it might provide the services in the
facilities of a state or local welfare agency. When governments contract
for services the client may be unaware of who is providing them; but
regardless of who pays the workers' salaries, public services such as job
search assistance are provided under the auspices of state or local government and financed by taxpayers. Government remains responsible
for the character and quality of the services and is ultimately accountable to the client and to the taxpayer.[1]

Who provides the service may be of less interest to clients than their
judgment about the kind of treatment they get and the quality of the service they receive. But for politicians, taxpayers, and students of public
management, the question of who provides the service is of significant
interest. States are increasingly exercising the option to contract out, and
many advocates of this strategy see a strong relationship between who
delivers the service and its cost, quality, and character. As state and local
governments make important decisions about what to provide in-house
and what to outsource, they are making judgments about the likely performance of different kinds of providers. But there are other important
considerations in sponsorship, especially for human services. Govern-

ment agencies, nonprofits, and for-profit firms may differ not only in their capacities for appropriate performance, but also in the values and norms that attend their work. Whether the blurring of sectoral boundaries is likely also to blur those distinctions is an important question.

States and localities have contracted out for provision of services in a wide range of areas for a long time. Strong arguments are advanced in favor of governments' purchasing services rather than providing them in-house. Nonprofits in human services have worked cooperatively with government under a variety of arrangements to provide needed expertise. New York City's Housing Preservation and Development Agency, for example, contracts with the Red Cross for emergency assistance to families who are burned out of their homes or otherwise removed from dangerous housing situations. The Red Cross has recognized expertise in dealing with human tragedy and helping families in short-term emergency situations. The public trusts its motives and competence. These are important virtues for garnering public support, especially in dealing with sensitive human services.

Recently, a loosening of federal constraints and an increase in the size of the market (and in the size of caseloads needing service) has encouraged the entrance of large for-profit firms in a number of human services markets. Their presence is changing the environment profoundly. For-profit firms operating in human services markets receive a mixed reception. They are welcomed for the cost savings and efficiencies they promise, but their presence also causes trepidation. The increasing commercialization of human services markets is changing the meaning of public service and the nature of those held accountable for promoting the public interest. With the increasing retreat of government providers and threats to the survival of many traditional nonprofits, marketization of human services poses new risks to vulnerable populations that depend on them and to the nonprofit industry, which is heavily invested in servicing them. These developments promise to change the role and responsibilities of government and to affect long-standing relationships among the three sectors of the economy.

Public-private partnerships operate in virtually all service areas and at every level of government; they have in the United States for centuries. However, government is no longer merely a buyer of a standardized product like pencils or blankets. Its private partners are now engaged in producing products and services that are not strictly off the shelf. Government has participated in the creation and coordination of markets and market relationships that did not previously exist—from weapons to social services. "As a result the government is no longer a buyer dealing at arm's length with a seller but a partner in a virtually seamless, mutually dependent interrelationship. These growing public-private ties, including substantial links with the nonprofit sector for social services, have blurred the boundaries among the sectors, making it harder to distinguish between public and private accountability."[2] Although contracting and competition have increasingly been promoted as ways to escape from alleged governmental pathologies—the inherent bureaucratic and civil service constraints on efficiency and change—Kettl reminds us of the irony that these relationships have brought both sectors closer together. "Instead of *privatizing the public sector,* the federal government's management strategies have tended to *governmentalize the private sector.*"[3] The same can be said of state and local arrangements.

State and local agencies, nonprofit organizations, and private firms are increasingly operating in local markets, sometimes together. While each performs in accordance with contractual agreements as an agent of the state, its comparative advantages are often quite different. Local community-based organizations (CBOs), for example, have deep knowledge of their communities, including the needs of their residents and the resources that are available locally. Private for-profit firms have access to capital and can often move quickly to build the infrastructure to serve large numbers of clients. However, as each has a unique mission and operates under different governance arrangements, their funding and organizational constraints may vary. New contracting arrangements that force nonprofits to compete with for-profits can change their priorities, requiring them to choose between meeting the market test and maintaining commitments to their primary mission. New contractual requirements and competitive demands are altering the way they do business and, in many cases, whether they can do business at all.

Devolution of authority and reduced mandates from the federal government have accelerated contracting in state and local governments, especially in human services. These trends have been accompanied by a resurgence of confidence in the performance of the private sector[4] and have been effecting important changes at the state and local level. While governments at all levels have contracted out for a wide range of goods and services for decades—and in some cases for more than a century[5]— a marked change in the nature and scope of services targeted for outsourcing has begun to characterize state and local service delivery. Some of the acceleration in these practices has been induced by political pressures to reduce the size of government. Additional pressures have come from a desire at the local level to reduce costs, improve performance, and circumvent the constraints on flexibility and innovation imposed by public employees unions. Perhaps most important, however, has been a change in philosophy about what governments can do best and what the private and nonprofit sectors can do better. Some of the rhetoric is highly ideological, but much is surprisingly pragmatic: local governments are looking for solutions that reduce their costs, improve their service options, and circumvent bureaucratic obstacles. One government welfare official in New York City described it this way: "Government is best at setting outcomes, designing policy, and overseeing and supervising performance. It's not great at operational activities and service delivery. There are simply too many processes and inefficiencies. Contracting is better, cheaper, and more flexible, allowing you to add and contract when needed."[6]

Whatever the merits of these views, both those that respond to the political pressures to reduce government employment and those that have redefined the functions of government, these changes are taking place with little systematic monitoring of: 1) the level, character, and distribution of contracting out at all levels of government; 2) the effects on costs, quality, and performance of these new delivery arrangements; 3) changes in the functions, roles, and responsibilities of the sectors; and 4) resulting shifts in the distribution of talent and capacity among the sectors. Further, changes in governance implied by the shift in the locus of public service provision may affect communities in different ways, especially by the potential threats that private for-profit providers may impose on CBOs that have sprung up as significant providers of local services in many neighborhoods. Changes in the size and direction of service delivery have increased, but little systematic research has yet sought to evaluate the impact of these changes.[7]

Background

Welfare reform generated a particularly contentious national policy debate.[8] However, it had the virtue of arriving at a time when the dual goals of devolution and reinvention had become national truisms, embraced by Republicans and new Democrats alike. Many political factors have accelerated the desires of state and local governments to contract out recently, not least of which is the pressure to reduce the size of government. In human services, however, the practice is at least a century old. Purchase of services from nonprofits, in particular, has its roots as early as the colonial era, when the country's poor laws and state and local emphasis on "outdoor relief" resulted in local authorities' "auctioning off" the poor—aged and orphans among them—to voluntary agencies or private individuals for care. These various arrangements, which included public subsidies to private charitable organizations, continued in different forms through the 1930s, when depression-era legislation increased the level of support provided from public institutions. Contracting out to voluntary agencies, often religious, to provide support and services—often "rehabilitation"—is an American tradition of long standing. Various forms of voluntary assistance developed through the church, mutual-benefit societies, and private philanthropy, supplementing a very modest assumption of government responsibility.

Through much of American history the balance between public and private systems has shifted as the merits of one or the other prevailed.[9] In the early part of the twentieth century, in reaction to perceived abuses in private contracting systems, public purchase of services gave way to direct subsidies to voluntary welfare organizations. Voluntary and religious organizations met the needs of limited government's roles in poverty alleviation until the Great Depression, when government stepped in to meet the national emergency. Even with greater government assumption of many social welfare functions, however, the nonprofit sector has remained a key service provider in dozens of social welfare functions, financed with public funds as well as private philanthropy. While the relative importance of different sources of funds has shifted over time with changing federal policies, programs, and budgetary commitments, government funds represented a majority of the revenues of social service nonprofits as recently as 1997.[10]

The private sector, too, has been providing goods and services to government as early as colonial times. George Washington complained about private suppliers who were slow to deliver and often stole. Waste, fraud, and abuse in defense contracts began even before the nation did.

The United States has always had a smaller public sector, less public ownership of production, and a smaller social sector than other nations. Following the American lead, countries throughout the world are now experimenting with market-based public management solutions for the ills of bureaucracy. Though the management reforms around the world show significant convergence, in the United States, where "use of nongovernmental partners [forms] an essential and perhaps irreversible part of the governance system,"[11] they reflect a deep and pervasive distrust of government and long-standing preference for markets.

The balance between private and public providers in the social welfare arena began to change in the 1980s.[12] Marketization of social welfare services is important because shifting emphasis in the relationships between the three sectors of the economy is likely to favor different values and norms in operation.[13] The choice of sponsorship is more than a question of relative efficiency in provision, which is a major argument for contracting out. Government policies expressed in contractual agreements with providers may govern provision, whoever sponsors the service. But evaluating changes in the direction and extent of private contracting, especially in human services, is important because relative changes are likely to be accompanied by "changes in the degree of equity, responsiveness, flexibility and liberty that one or another of these sectors promotes as dominant concerns."[14] Furthermore, accountability is more difficult to ensure when services are contracted than when government is the provider; and market pressures impose a discipline that creates a bias favoring some public goals over others. Equity and accountability, two important goals of a democratic state, are likely to take a back seat to cost and efficiency when market rules apply.

The unique role of the nonprofit sector in serving vulnerable populations is an important factor in its historic relationship as a partner of government in social welfare. Maintaining the health of the nonprofit sector may necessitate preserving its unique community and charitable values, values that may be compromised when nonprofits play by market rules.[15] When nonprofits must capitulate to larger collective mandates of government they risk losing their raison d'être as community institutions.[16] Nonprofits vary in their degree of dependence on government for resources, and their structure and organization reflect this variation. The most recent data available show that social services organizations received more than 52 percent of their income in 1997 from government funding in the form of grants and contracts. This makes them dependent on government demands and subject to the vicissitudes of policy changes and public budgets.[17]

Community-based organizations, many of which have been central to community development in poor urban areas, represent much of the social capital and civic infrastructure in many of these communities. They have strong claims as community providers that reflect deep value commitments to clients and strong connections to their target communities. When they are confronted by changing relations with government or lose in the competitive arena in the provision of human service delivery, a great deal more is lost than services. Many of these organizations allow for community participation and broader community investment through the jobs they provide, the income they spend, and the contributions they make to neighborhood development.

The most valuable contributions of CBOs come from their local expertise. The services they provide would be different if product standardization were required to achieve economies. While the caseloads of many CBOs are small, their service packages are tailored to the special needs of the clients they serve. Some community organizations have particular expertise and experience with special groups—substance abusers, ex-offenders, victims of domestic abuse, or multiproblem families. Historically, these organizations have been important providers of employment and training. The provision in contracting arrangements for the participation of small but specialized community-based providers may have important effects on the quality and appropriateness of the services available.

Welfare reform has shifted the emphasis of public assistance programs from income maintenance to work. However, clients differ in their degree of job readiness and in the obstacles they face in entering the labor market. Many nonprofit providers have long histories of service to disadvantaged populations that exhibit multiple barriers to self-sufficiency. The "work-first" imperative embedded in the 1996 legislation eschews, in large part, longer and more intensive education and training services in favor of direct job placement and short-term job readiness skills. Federal mandates to the states for caseload engagement have put significant pressure on state and local governments to meet placement targets. These imperatives have been passed along to private contractors. The responses of these contractors and their effects on clients and communities reveal some of the virtues and limitations of market-based arrangements in human services. Furthermore, how these arrangements change the behavior, capacity, and roles of the different players in a multisectored human services industry bears significant scrutiny.

The legitimate role of government is another concern. Loss of capacity is but one concern. When governments relinquish their roles in providing services, they relinquish considerable discretion and accountability to third parties. In some areas of service delivery the consequences of this shift in governance pose few serious risks. In areas where vulnerable clients must rely on the discretion of third parties, the consequences can be grave. Growth in contracting must be accompanied by an equal growth in government's ability to manage and monitor contractor behavior, but there are indications that these developments do not necessarily coincide.[18]

Thus this reconnaissance reflects on the opportunities and dangers that attend a service area undergoing significant reorganization under a new set of rules—rules that may elevate market benefits above other important public values. How well public purposes are achieved and how effectively private contractors can balance public service goals with private benefits under these new arrangements are important subjects of the inquiry. My findings provide some broad generalizations about the changing nature of sectoral relations under these conditions.

Why Contract?

Government contracting is a long-standing practice, but the enthusiasm with which it is currently embraced reflects more recent antecedents. The presidency of Ronald Reagan marked the beginning of a transformation in most Americans' view of government. Conservative analysts of the 1980s portrayed government as the problem rather than the solution. During these years policymakers sought to reduce the size and activities of the federal government, and by extension local governments, through reduced revenues and retrenchment. Reducing the size of government was an explicit ambition and a yardstick by which public officials were ultimately judged. The expanded role of the state that had begun in response to the Great Depression came to a halt during the Reagan revolution, and the stage was set for a new view of service provision in the 1990s.

The enduring conflict between the desire for public services and the hostility to government bureaucracies reflects a fundamental ambivalence about the appropriate scope of government activity in the United States. This conflict has created what Lester Salamon has called "third party government," where considerable numbers of activities funded and directed by the government are carried out by other institutions, which deliver many of the services with considerable discretion about who is served and how.[19] This puts government in the position of operating by remote control, relying on other entities to deliver the services that government has authorized.[20] Even during periods of significant fiscal retrenchment, nonprofits have remained important partners of government in the delivery of services—especially in the provision of employment and training.

Current debates about contracting derive from efforts not so much to circumvent government as to transform it. Many recent reforms rest on arguments central to the "new public management." These reforms represent efforts to reshape and improve governance through a reexamination of how the relationships among the state, society, and the market are ordered.[21] "The management reform movement builds on the notion that good governance—the sorting out of mission, role, capacity, and relationships—is a necessary (if insufficient) condition for economic prosperity and social stability."[22]

Calls to reinvent government are reflected in the popular literature and Clinton-era initiatives such as the National Performance Review (NPR). While the NPR was highly politicized and its accomplishments continue to be debated, it grappled more or less with the big issues of the management reform movement. The effort emphasized approaches that worked better and cost less; a consideration of what government ought to do; and the use of technologies of the new information age that could improve government efficiency. These new emphases at the federal level were accompanied by what Kettl calls a "subtle revolution quietly transforming American management."[23] With growing devolution of federal authority to the states, the states found themselves increasingly responsible for administration and policymaking. Welfare reform is perhaps the most visible example, but a myriad of formerly federal directives in multiple functional areas like Medicaid and environmental protection have given states and localities new responsibilities and discretion.

In 1996 welfare reform came around at just the right time to ride the crest of the public management reform wave. Current reform efforts—in which contracting and other forms of privatization are central—have taken on pragmatic dimensions at the state and local level.[24] Pragmatism and accountability for results drive local officials to select strategies capable of getting things done. Citizens respond to accomplishments that cost less, that are more effective and more responsive. Republicans and New Democrats see markets as an additional weapon in their public service arsenals, and the increasing use of contracts reflects their growing popularity at the local level. Mayors and county executives across the country, from New York and Philadelphia to Indianapolis and San Diego, have contracted out just about every service. Collectively, the reforms shaped by devolution and the new public management seek to replace bureaucratic models, characterized by "traditional rule based authority-driven processes with market based, competition-driven tactics."[25]

Advocates of contracting out point to its potential to improve government performance by exploiting market arrangements. The promise is for lower costs, greater efficiencies, and more innovation and flexibility. Contracting allows local governments to circumvent the myriad rules and processes, which represent significant costs and constraints on operations. While there are great examples of highly skilled public managers who creatively circumvent the inherent constraints of public bureaucracies, contracting allows public officials to claim success in reducing the size of government while escaping from the rules on how services are organized and provided that are imposed by public employees unions.[26]

Contracting may be the mantra, but it is competition that drives reforms in service delivery. The service provider need not be a private contractor. A competitive bidding process may allow public agencies to choose among a number of providers—public agencies included—who have incentives to organize production in the most efficient manner, thereby producing the lowest bid for the desired services. Cities like San Diego and Indianapolis have improved performance by having public agencies bid competitively along with private contractors for delivering city services.

San Diego modeled its efforts to bring competition into county service provision after the success achieved in Indianapolis under Mayor Stephen Goldsmith. San Diego County sold its solid waste system and outsourced information technology and telecommunications services and welfare-to-work services.[27] All depended on competitive bidding, and public agencies competed. County teams won six of seven other competitions in various service areas and continued to provide the service; the competitive environment presumably induced increased efficiencies and incentives to keep service levels high and costs low even in public agencies.[28]

Including public agencies in the competitive bidding process sensitizes public managers to the structure of the agencies' costs and to the characteristics of the production process. It requires cooperation between labor and management that can improve morale and precipitate changes in work rules and motivation among public employees. Some cities have even created competition among public agencies for contracts, and others are engaging in what is known as managed competition, where multiple providers deliver services together in the same market. This was the model in all the cases studied for this book. Welfare-to-work contracts were bid competitively, but private for-profit, nonprofit, and public agencies, in some cases, were all part of the mix for the contracts covering a specific geographical region within the jurisdiction. Competition works here on two levels, both at the bidding stage and at the performance stage, where competing organizations are continually being compared with one another. Firms are constantly on their toes since they lack even the temporary complacency of a monopolist who has a sole-source contract. In most cases contract renewals depend on the contractor's meeting specific performance standards, with the expectation that when caseloads decline, only the best performers will be retained.

If public officials design a performance-based contract, where outcomes, or at least outputs, are properly specified, contractors have still greater incentives to maximize profits by providing a given level of performance at the lowest cost. Contracting benefits from these arrangements, however, only in the presence of competent firms and a competitive market. These conditions do not always exist. Government actions can exacerbate weak markets by choosing a sole source contract or by allowing unrestrained competition to gradually reduce the numbers of potential providers. Government can find itself captive to monopolists— the avoidance of which is a major motivation to contract in the first place. Only through a process of regular contract reauthorization can public officials hold a sole-source contractor accountable to a desired level of performance. Ascertaining an appropriate performance level, however, can be difficult if there are no competitors to establish an appropriate benchmark. The lack of clear benchmarks represents a principal difficulty for judging the performance of public monopolies.

Contracting has other virtues, however. In new service areas, or for services for which government has less expertise than private providers, contracting allows governments to benefit from the experience and knowledge they do not possess in-house. In areas where there are rapidly changing approaches or new technology, governments can exploit private competence without committing to long-term labor or capital investments. Some large contracts in human services began as efforts to take advantage of emerging technological expertise and hardware not yet available to state and local governments.

MAXIMUS, a current behemoth in the welfare reform business, made its name initially by applying its technology and management information systems to collecting child-support payments in many states. Similarly, Lockheed Martin IMS won a number of large contracts to provide electronic transfers of benefits for public assistance clients in a number of states.[29] These were areas where government technological capacity and expertise were inadequate, program performance was generally poor, and efforts to upgrade public systems capacity posed labor, budget, and management problems.[30] While not all these arrangements proved successful, technology and large systems management capacity keep a foot in the door through which large national firms have an opportunity to gain a foothold in human services around the country. With the passage of welfare reform, a number of large national players were well positioned to enter the market.

Contracting out has considerable appeal, but it also carries risks. Contractors may fail to perform; they may engage in fraud and corruption or fail to treat clients equitably. Contracting appeals to governments because of its potential for them to offload functions or to build capacity when special circumstances require it. This was the case for local governments contracting for welfare-to-work services. But ensuring improved performance through contracting is not self-regulating. If contracts specify the inputs desired and the means to be used (what Robert Behn calls regulatory contracts), they risk inhibiting innovations in program design or production that might improve cost effectiveness.[31] Ensuring compliance requires that significant resources be allocated to auditing contractor behavior with no guarantee that even strict compliance will result in the desired outcomes.

Performance or incentive-based contracts pay for results. In the welfare-to-work industry, however, most contracts are still structured for cost reimbursement or fixed price. Only 20 percent of all Temporary Assistance to Needy Families (TANF) contracts in 2001 were incentive based in any way.[32] Some, like those used in the welfare contracts in Milwaukee and New York, offer a maximum payment per client when all of a number of milestones are met. In New York, for example, a fixed amount is paid when a client is placed in a job, with additional amounts when clients are placed in good jobs of reasonable duration.

Thus premiums are paid when a client stays on the job for three to six months. Additional amounts accrue if the wages are in excess of a minimum or if a job results in a client's exit from the welfare roles. Payments are made only if job placement is achieved, regardless of the efforts (or resources) expended on behalf of a client.[33] These kinds of contracts provide incentives for contractors to achieve desired results, but their success depends on identifying the right kinds of results to reward.

Developing the right measures of performance is no easy job; considerable knowledge and experience are necessary to ensure that measures of service performance are properly specified, measurable, and verifiable. For a routine service like refuse collection, specifying the dimensions in tons of garbage or blocks covered per day and adding measures for quality dimensions like timeliness, courtesy, and cleanliness may be relatively routine. For human services, or services that are relatively new or customized, or where performance expectations are not altogether settled, contract design becomes a difficult and resource-intensive activity. The choice of measures is critical, and often when a jurisdiction contracts a service for the first time, several rounds of contracts may be necessary before optimal measures can be developed.

New York City has a reengineered welfare system. Its former Human Resources (HRA) administrator, Jason Turner, was severely criticized by the city comptroller (and the courts) for hiring consultants from MAXIMUS in the early stages of contract design who later bid for and won a contract.[34] MAXIMUS, however, had had contracting experience in numerous jurisdictions around the country—experience that the city needed to design its performance-based contract. Whatever the propriety of the relationship, the city clearly needed the expertise.

Recognizing the critical role of contract design to success in the city's new performance based system, HRA enlisted Richard Bonamarte, the city's chief procurement officer in the mayor's office before the city's decision to reengineer its welfare delivery system, to help design the contract concepts. Learning from the abysmal performance of historic NYC Department of Employment contracts, HRA aimed to eliminate line-item payments in favor of more limited but explicit payment for clearly identified outcomes. The key decisions related to how much to pay for different kinds of outcomes—placement and retention.

The dilemmas Bonamarte faced are instructive. Paying too much for initial placements and too little for job retention (or quality jobs) encourages contractors to provide little service or effort to find quality jobs in which the client is likely to stay for any length of time. "Contractors' propensity is to do as little as possible."[35] But placing too much of the payment at the back end may impede the cash flow over time and cripple contractors' ability to stay afloat as they absorb expenses while they wait for payment. "It's a balancing act . . . balancing the milestone payments in order to provide a flow of cash over the contract. Back ending too much of the payment cripples their ability to perform. The contract design needs to balance optimizing cash flow with setting milestones at the desired outcomes."[36] The problem, Bonamarte argued, was providing the right balance between the incentives in the design to ensure the correct emphasis on the desired outcomes and ensuring the fiscal stability of the contracting organizations. "It would be good to be able to tweak them [the contracts] along the way when we had learned a lot. But when you make a material change to the contract terms, the lawyers say you have to rebid it. Thus, the process is half art and half science."[37]

The challenges in rewarding providers for employment placement of low-income groups are legendary.[38] Is the desired result job placement? Retention? Economic well-being? Are there different results that might be desired for different types of clients? Are the same results to be expected from a high-school dropout as from a client with a high-school diploma? Each of these questions implies a differently designed contract likely to result in profound variations in outcome and in contractor behavior. For example, if the result depends more on the characteristics of the client than on the behavior of the contractor, perversions of contractual intent can be induced. Contractors may seek clients more likely to succeed than those with greater (and more costly) needs. Performance-based contracts demand considerable capacity on the part of the contractors to track and verify client success. Contract monitoring functions require significant resource investments by the jurisdiction.

Successful contracting requires government officials to be smart buyers and good contract managers.[39] Being a smart buyer begins well before selection of the proper contract design, when local officials make judgments about what functions are most suitable candidates for contracting out. San Diego's chief administrative officer, Lawrence Prior, used Indianapolis mayor Goldsmith's Yellow Pages test to choose competitive targets: if the telephone book listed five or more private firms selling the same service as a county agency, that service was added to a priority list.[40]

Contracting for results requires selecting service areas where multiple contractors are available (to avoid the risk of replacing one monopoly with another) and the result desired can be well specified in advance, measurable, and verifiable. Efforts to reduce the risks of contracting involve considerable costs. Transaction costs are high to perform the multiple functions of selecting, monitoring, and evaluating vendors. These costs include the maintenance of internal capacity—talent and expertise that are necessary to make good decisions or to change vendors or contracting arrangements when they are not. Because contracting skill develops over time with experience, especially concerning new functions, having a staff of managers with the necessary knowledge and expertise, which develop over multiple contracting cycles, is critical to ensuring performance and cost savings. Because such talent is scarce and public salaries are low for such managers, vendors often have a comparative advantage in attracting them.

New York City's chief procurement officer who was responsible for designing the current welfare-to-work contracts has recently left the city to join the management team of one of the prime contractors, Wildcat Service Corporation. His exit from government is typical of many experienced managers. This brain drain has many antecedents, but when private contractors compete, they compete with one another for talent as well as contracts; the result in any case may be reduced government capacity both to produce the service itself and to manage the procurement and contract monitoring functions well.[41]

Contracting is popular because it fulfills many of the political and economic interests of both public managers and citizens, but it is hard to do well—especially in providing human services. Public, nonprofit, and private providers have different comparative advantages. Evaluating the relative risks and rewards of various arrangements and choosing carefully may represent the most important functions of public officials considering outsourcing.

Contracting Out in States and Localities

Contracting for services reflects the pragmatism of mayors and county executives around the country, but it also signals a more generalized rethinking of the role of government. The past few decades have witnessed an overall increase in contracting by state and local governments. Not surprisingly, contracting varies significantly by service area. Prisons and criminal justice systems are still largely public, while heavy construction is almost always private. Human services has a long tradition of contracting, but recently the contracts going to for-profit providers have increased dramatically. Employment and job training contracts have experienced dramatic shifts in the character of providers, especially since the passage of the Personal Responsibility and Work Opportunity Reconciliation Act (PRWORA).

The magnitude and characteristics of the changes in state and local government contracting reflect its importance as a management tool, especially for local governments. Surprisingly, however, data sources on state and local contracting are quite limited. Comprehensive national survey data have been scarce, discontinuous, and usually not comparable from one survey to another. Five nationwide surveys are available with some relevant data points and some coverage of years from 1982 to 1999.[42] These data, though flawed, reveal some important trends about the percentage of governments contracting out a given service, those involved in contracting at all, and the use of public employees for delivering public services.

Subnational jurisdictions are contracting more. All the surveys found that most jurisdictions are contracting out more in most service areas. The International City/County Management Association (ICMA) reported that contracting increased between 1982 and 1997, with the percent of cities and counties surveyed who contract out increasing in most service areas. A better and more recent survey by ICMA, 1988–97, shows that more jurisdictions were contracting out to provide services in most service areas. During the most recent period, 1992–97, when the survey is most comparable, there is also an increase in jurisdictions contracting out. However, the rate of increase decreased somewhat during this period, which is also the shortest period surveyed.

Counties, too, rely more on contracting for services. A National Bureau of Economic Research (NBER) study using census data confirmed that from 1987 to 1992 the counties contracting experienced a rate of increase that ranged from 38 percent to 206 percent over the period, but because initial levels were low, this represented only an increase of 0.7–6.4 percentage points. In 1987 counties delivered more than three times more of the reported services than contractors. Five years later, they delivered less than twice as many. Thus more jurisdictions contract their services and do so over an increasing number of service areas. Perhaps most significant, for services not offered in the earlier period that were offered in 1992 (most likely to be new services), a higher percentage was provided by private contractors (4.3 percent) than by county employees (3.2 percent). The rest were likely provided by another jurisdiction or other form of privatization such as franchise or vouchers.

Additional survey results provide more support. The Mercer Group found the percentage of local governments contracting out some portion of a given service area had increased from 1987 to 1995 for all services covered by their survey. Increases ranged from 31 percent to 166 percent, and from 2 to 20 percentage points for all twenty-two services surveyed. States surveyed in 1997 by the Council of State Governments (CSG) found a large majority of respondents (58.6 percent) reporting increased privatization activity and 55.2 percent reporting an expectation that privatization activities would continue to increase over the next five years.

Overall, a recent (1998) National Association of Counties (NAC) survey reported that 84 percent of counties provide at least one major service through contracting. One year later that figure had increased to 90 percent—a 6 percentage point increase in a single year. These trends in increased contracting obviously vary by service area, but even in a period where service expenditures have increased for state and local governments, they have increased more for those *not* performed by public employees (13 percent as against 28 percent.) Thus, despite the lack of data or comparability between sources, all surveys indicate an increase in jurisdictions contracting out regardless of the unit of analysis (state, county, city, or some combination). These data also show a general increase across most service areas even while their rates of change and actual percentage point increases may vary. Whatever their flaws, existing data are helpful in estimating the direction and magnitudes of change over the past two decades. Further research will be necessary to strengthen the data, make them more comparable, and monitor them over time. Existing surveys suffer in a number of dimensions: response rates are sometimes low, questions are often not comparable with earlier surveys, and service areas considered have changed from survey to survey.

One recent analysis, however, cautions careful interpretation of the data. Increases in the number of jurisdictions contracting and the number of services being contracted obscure some important trends. Recent work by Warner and Hebdon,[43] for example, shows that the aggregate trends mask considerable mobility in local government behaviors over time. Warner and Hebdon discovered increasing mobility and complexity of local contracting-out decisions. Though overall contracting out is increasing, Warner and Hebdon found that many jurisdictions that have found the contracting experience unsatisfactory reverted to public provision—a phenomenon they describe as reverse privatization. Further, they demonstrate that local governments are using a broad set of service restructuring alternatives in addition to privatization.[44] Three recent questions Warner and Hebdon had included in the NAC survey revealed that "contracting back in" is also a big piece of the story, but until recently its significance was overlooked by public policy scholars. If local governments find that unsatisfactory contracting outcomes are a significant problem, they might need to maintain capacity to resume services in-house or at least to restructure service delivery in other ways.

No surveys evaluate the frequency or growth in contracting out specifically for the employment and training function, but these services have a long history of being outsourced by state and local governments, especially since 1973, when the Comprehensive Employment and Training Act (CETA) poured federal resources into the employment training industry and allocated large sums to states and localities. Many employment and training services under the act were provided under contract to nonprofits and, less often, to for-profit organizations. Since then contracting for these services has been *de rigueur.* In New York City alone, as early as 1986 some agencies responsible for employment and training provided no direct services at all. Virtually all employment and training managed by the NYC Department of Employment was provided by purchase of service agreements with outside providers.[45] Most of these providers were nonprofits. Like other human services, employment and training services are now increasingly being contracted to private for-profit providers.

Data on the growth in nonprofit and for-profit roles in the employment and job training industry are limited, but available data come from the U.S. Census Bureau.[46] Between 1986/87 and 1995/96, for-profits had a higher growth rate than nonprofits in all but two years. Annual rates of growth of for-profits had greatly exceeded that of nonprofits by 1996. For-profits had successfully tripled their revenues in the industry from 1987, capturing as much as 39 percent of that held by the previously dominant nonprofits.[47] Their continued growth as serious players in the industry since the passage of PRWORA in 1996, as welfare-to-work contracting has become the norm for state and local jurisdictions, is notable.

A recent survey by the U.S. General Accounting Office on all fifty states and the ten counties with the largest federal TANF funding allocations (in the states where TANF is administered locally) finds contracting of services to be extensive. Contracting out for TANF-funded services exceeded $1.5 billion in federal and state funds for 2001.[48] Every state (with the exception of South Dakota) and the District of Columbia contracts for TANF services.[49] About 88 percent of total funds contracted by state governments and 73 percent of the state-level contracts are with nonprofits, and the rest are with for-profit providers. Several states have large portions of for-profit providers: in eight states at least half of the contracted funds are with for-profit organizations. Nineteen states have more than 25 percent of their contracted funds with for-profits. Most provide education and training and job placement and support services to promote job entry or retention.[50] Like other areas of service delivery, welfare to work is experiencing dramatic increases in the use of contractors, especially for-profit firms.

The reconnaissance undertaken for this book examined the growth rates and explored the business strategies in some nationwide firms delivering employment and social services, especially to welfare clients. These data, too, reveal that private contracting is expanding in many states, cities, and counties and that the contractors are broadening both the size of their contracts and the range of services they provide in greater numbers of jurisdictions across the country.[51]

CHAPTER THREE

Reforming Welfare Services through Contracting: Motivations and Expectations

Outsourcing appeals to local public officials. It meets many of their political and management objectives, bringing business-like practices to government and responding to public pressures to reduce costs and public employment. Welfare reform has provided an additional impetus. Two major legislative changes have conditioned the way states and localities restructured their job readiness, placement, and employment services to welfare recipients. The first and most important was the 1996 Personal Responsibility and Work Opportunity Reconciliation Act (PRWORA). The second was the Workforce Investment Act (WIA) of 1998. PRWORA and the Temporary Assistance to Needy Families (TANF) program that it created gave states great flexibility in the design of programs and services while holding them accountable for moving substantial portions of their caseloads to employment or work-related activities: 25 percent in FY 1997; 40 percent in FY2000; and 50 percent in FY 2002 and thereafter. (Currently debated proposals for reauthorization would increase the level to 70 percent in future years.)

These federal mandates created opportunity and incentive for local governments to provide services differently. State programs immediately refocused on engaging welfare recipients and applicants in preparing for and finding employment. The "work-first" philosophy of most states' responses required a new configuration of states' welfare services and greater willingness to seek or expand the use of contractors to provide them.

At the same time that welfare services were being reengineered, the Labor Department's new WIA legislation made new demands on states for employment and training funding. Under the previous Job Training Partnership Act (JTPA), training grants were provided to states with specific provisions for serving low-income and welfare recipients. WIA required states to redesign their employment and training systems and manage them in new ways. The most important changes were for the establishment of local work-force investment areas and local work-force investment boards to oversee the design and establishment of "one-stop" centers where customers could be assessed, obtain information, and receive job search and placement assistance along with career counseling. WIA funds are available for various services to many categories of adults and youth, but welfare recipients and low-income individuals are given priority for intensive services. State and local boards were free to contract out their "one-stop centers," and they in turn could subcontract for additional supplemental services. Further, eligible individuals could use funds from an individual training account (ITA) to seek specialized training from vendors that the state had certified in their local area. WIA differs principally from its predecessors in its reduced funding levels and the resulting emphasis on shorter-term training and other less costly alternatives.

Thus TANF required a policy shift that required states and localities to rethink services and their delivery, while the WIA required new delivery mechanisms. Both legislative initiatives allowed the states and the localities to which they devolved authority considerable latitude in accomplishing their mandates, giving them incentive and considerable discretion to reengineer welfare-to-work systems.

The result has favored contracting. There has been wide variation in the design of delivery systems, the number and character of providers, and the terms under which they work (see box 1-1). Some localities, like Houston, merged their systems for job training, using contractors to serve both TANF clients and others eligible under the WIA. Others, like Milwaukee, San Diego, and New York have different initial points of entry for welfare clients than for others served by the one-stop centers. Even in these cases, however, contractors may serve both TANF and WIA clients. Milwaukee has contracted eligibility determination and assessment, job readiness services, and placement. San Diego and Houston have contracted for case management. New York has separate contractors for assessment and placement and engages still others to provide employment services and placement for clients with more significant needs. Recently the city has entered into an additional set of contracts with private vendors to serve clients with special needs.

In addition, each jurisdiction I studied remunerates its contractors differently. Houston pays cost of services to a certain maximum. New York, San Diego, and Milwaukee pay for performance, with different amounts allocated as clients reach different milestones, beginning with job placement, and with additional amounts paid for the duration and quality of jobs. Thus, for example, New York provides a minimum payment for a job placement and additional increments when clients can be certified to have been on the job for three months or for six months and still more if the job pays high wages (currently above $9.00 an hour) or results in an exit from the welfare rolls. In contrast, in Houston a contractor might be paid for client services even if a job placement fails to endure. No payment would be made if a client failed to find employment operating under a performance-based contract in New York or Milwaukee.

State and local officials have a range of motivations and expectations when they choose to contract out their services. Long lists of benefits and costs are catalogued in the literature.[1] However, states and localities contemplating the outsourcing of welfare reform initiatives vary in their motivations and in their expectations about what they can hope to achieve. Since most of the potential benefits of outsourcing come as much from creating competitive pressures as they do from relieving governments from activities they have difficulty in providing well, the development of multiple competent competitors is critical for privatizing services. All the cases we analyzed chose multiple providers, and the distribution of contract dollars in each site reflects the significance of the private sector among them (see figure 3-1).[2]

Not all states and localities around the country made the same choices. In Florida and Arizona, for example, a number of counties chose sole-source contracts with private for-profit vendors.[3] Since I was as interested in the impact of competition as in contracting, however, I did not include any of these cases in my reconnaissance.[4]

Government: Changing Roles and Behavior in Four Jurisdictions

In each of the jurisdictions studied, the motivation for restructuring the service delivery system varied somewhat, reflecting local political cultures

Figure 3-1. *Dividing up Total Contract Dollars: Percentage of Contracts by Contractor Type in Four Cities, 2001*

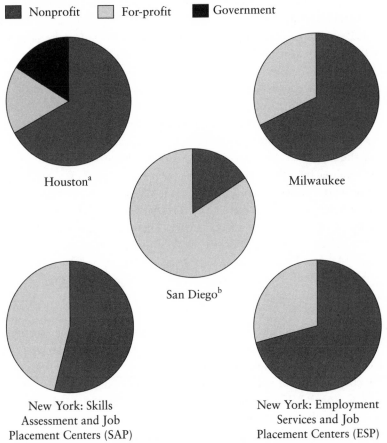

a. Government contracts discontinued in 2002 due to problems with accounting system.
b. Government amount not reflected.
Sources: Contract information provided by the Houston Department of Human Services, Gulf Coast Workforce Board; Wisconsin Department of Workforce Development, Office of Contracts; New York City Comptroller's Office; and County of San Diego, Contract Operations.

and variations in philosophy and executive leadership. The federal government now drives most of the opportunities for innovation created at the state and local level through grants and contracts. Changes in service delivery systems are easier to make when implementing new programs, where it is easier to avoid confrontations and resistance from recalcitrant bureaucracies that are tied to old processes and job descriptions. PRWORA (and the recently implemented WIA) provided the opportunity to redesign service delivery systems, and each jurisdiction studied took a different route. All jurisdictions contracted out for services and included private for-profit firms in the mix, however (see figure 3-1).

In New York, for example, contracts were very comprehensive and included two types of services. The first undertook initial client assessment and provided some short-term job-readiness and placement services; the second type provided services to those who failed to find employment after the four-week job-readiness program under the first contractor or whose needs were for some longer-term job training and placement services. These were known respectively as SAP and ESP contractors.[5] Each contractor selected serves clients in specific boroughs of the city, referred randomly by the city's Human Resources Administration (HRA). San Diego contracts for case management, assessment, and placement services, but a separate network provides more intensive services. Each contractor serves a specific region, with the result that four contractors serve the six regions in the county in the most recent round of contracts: two private, one nonprofit, and one county government provider. Milwaukee, through Wisconsin Works (W-2), contracted with five contractors, three nonprofits, one private provider, and a limited liability corporation of the YMCA in a regionally based delivery system like New York's.[6] The managed-competition model includes all services, including eligibility determination.[7] Houston contracted with one private, four nonprofits, and one public organization to run one-stop centers for TANF clients and others eligible under different Department of Labor titles in various parts of the county.[8]

All these jurisdictions refocused their services to welfare clients using a work-first approach, and all now use performance-based contracts with the exception of Houston, which retains contracts that pay, based on a cost-reimbursement model, to a certain maximum amount. Each was at a different point in its life cycle, with Milwaukee and San Diego into their second round of contracts under TANF and Houston and New York still in their first at the time of interview. Milwaukee and Houston had a particularly early start, taking advantage of federal waivers to experiment with some innovations before the passage of PRWORA.

Virtues of the Market

Public officials are eager to harness what they view as the virtues of the market, but not without restraint.[9] In theory they might have designed systems where contractors were free to recruit TANF clients.[10] But none did. No site in the study has introduced head-to-head competition for the initial enrollment of TANF clients.[11] Instead, contracting out allowed them to introduce competition through the request-for-proposal process. Further, most believed that the existence of multiple providers serving similar populations, in defined geographical areas, in the same market, would create sufficient competitive pressures to discipline their behavior. The discipline they sought was of two types: to reduce costs and improve performance. By tying payments to performance and allowing contractors latitude in how services were provided, the jurisdictions sought to increase performance and provide incentives for innovative programming. Most of the public officials interviewed believed that introducing market pressures of this type would be sufficient to provide incentives for performance and induce best practice. Since contracts are generally short (from one to three years) and renewable, comparative performance among current contractors would influence longer-term contracting decisions. This, they reasoned, would induce upfront capital investments in technology and management systems that would have long-term payoff.

Substituting multiple contractors for public provision avoids replacing one monopoly with another. The result allows public officials a system for benchmarking performance. Comparing the performance of each vendor means that contractors in these markets are always looking over their shoulders. While public officials in all the sites encouraged information sharing among their contractors, the implicit competition among them was expected to improve overall performance. Ensuring a mix of private, nonprofit, and, in one case, public providers was expected to improve them all.[12]

New York City, for example, has launched a new reporting system on line where contractors report performance, receive referrals, and receive feedback from a monthly EmploymentVendor*Stat Report. This monthly report compares the vendor's performance against all other providers by means of a ranking on all outcome measures. It imposes continuous pressure on the contractors to perform and highlights areas of weakness. In other sites, like San Diego, regular vendor meetings make public agencies and nonprofit organizations feel the direct competitive pressure that comes from being compared with private, profit-making, companies since performance data are available monthly. While no consistent qualitative outcome measures are used in any of the sites, public relations matters. Thus private companies need to be sensitive to public perceptions of how well they meet community needs and quality dimensions most often associated with nonprofit providers.[13]

Whatever the theoretical benefits local decisionmakers sought, practical problems associated with meeting new federal mandates required a new scale of operation, increased capacity, fast response, and arrangements that avoided the legal constraints to change that civil service unions impose. These immediate imperatives became the driving motivations for new contracting arrangements in the jurisdictions studied.

Scaling Up and Increasing Capacity

Before TANF, the Job Opportunities and Basic Skills Program (JOBS), under the Family Support Act of 1988, governed state welfare programs. JOBS imposed relatively modest federal requirements on states for client engagement in employment-related activities, with the dominant activity in many jurisdictions being work experience programs where eligible clients work for a minimum number of hours in public service jobs in public and nonprofit agencies. Under TANF, requirements for the engagement of clients are firm and sanctions for noncompliance severe. There exist fewer exemptions from eligibility, and engagement in employment-related activities is clearly defined. Perhaps most important, it imposed term limits of five years for the continuous receipt of assistance. States were free to impose more stringent limits, and Wisconsin and California chose two-year limits. New York chose five years, and Texas varies the limit from one to three years, depending on the work and education level of the client.[14]

Jurisdictions are mandated under TANF to involve increasing percentages of their caseloads in employment activities, and the primary goal for those who are able is direct job placement. These mandates have created extraordinary pressures on the service capacity of existing public agencies to find and engage large numbers of clients. The caseload to be served included both current recipients and applicants. San Diego's situation was typical. Compliance required the provision of intensive and extensive services on a large scale to serve two to three times more clients than were previously serviced. The management challenges were formidable. The new legislation created timing and capacity problems, what Joan Zinser, deputy director of San Diego's Health and Human Services Agency, called "the pig-in-the-python problem." Like other public officials interviewed, Ms. Zinser understood the difficulties of hiring sufficient staff and managers in time to meet the need to serve large numbers of new clients quickly. The staffing problem, however, was expected to be short term, since meeting the federal participation requirements would dramatically reduce the caseload over time. Thus the number of clients requiring services was expected to stabilize at a relatively modest level. Indeed, the number of clients to be served at the outset was 65,000, and by 2001 it had already fallen to 25,000.[15] Thus the ongoing public pressure to reduce public employees coupled with an expectation of continually declining caseloads over time provided the opportunity and motivation to contract.[16]

New York faced similar capacity pressures. Its caseloads from a combination of welfare clients, applicants, and eligible low-income adults rose from serving 4,000–5000 clients through the JTPA system to 40,000 under TANF and WIA.[17] Dramatic restructuring was felt to be necessary to quickly meet the demands. Previously, under JOBS and JTPA, the city had scores of contractors managed by its Department of Employment or the Human Resources Administration (HRA). Under TANF, the city moved all the contracts to HRA. In addition to awarding far fewer, but larger, contracts, city officials sought to circumvent what they expected to be a long process of review under a conventional RFP process. Indeed, they moved to a less public and more flexible process called negotiated acquisition.[18] In this process city officials would identify a group of the best-qualified providers in advance and invite them to bid. This provided flexibility in shaping contracts around contractor strengths. The precise nature of the contracts negotiated with individual providers varied somewhat, mostly in terms of payments. Despite the significant uproar this caused among advocates and good government groups, contrary to expectations, the city found that little time was saved. Indeed, the controversy elicited increased scrutiny of the final contracts in city council hearings and lengthy reviews (and calls for court action) by the NYC Comptroller's Office.[19]

Contracting was particularly attractive because of the flexibility it allows to adjust staffing needs to fluctuating demand. Clients who were easier to place—those with more work experience and education—were likely to be placed first and to constitute a declining proportion of the caseload over time. The challenges of reaching required federal placement targets for the harder to place—those with multiple barriers to employment—become ever more significant. Public officials in all the sites were thus motivated by a need for increased capacity as they initially engaged increasingly larger proportions of their caseloads each year. However, they also sought creative ways to induce innovation and motivation to deal with the increasing preponderance of the hard to serve.

Traditional ways of providing services were felt to be inadequate to the task. Reforming existing public agencies and their cultures to meet the new challenges was hard to do. Public officials were skeptical about their ability to restructure jobs and change incentives in existing welfare bureaucracies. They all feared the recalcitrance of public employees unions and did not expect much receptivity among current employees to meet changing needs. Contracting, therefore, allowed each to scale up quickly and to restructure delivery systems with maximum flexibility. Should demand for services decline over time, contracts could be renegotiated. In contrast, increased investment in in-house service provision would result in continuing cost commitments long after the need for additional staff had ended.[20]

Moving Fast

Building capacity represented a formidable challenge for public officials in each of the cases studied.[21] However, the need to do so quickly was probably an even more important incentive for turning to private contractors. Mark Hoover, New York City's first deputy commissioner of the Human Resources Administration and a veteran of Wisconsin's welfare reform efforts, described the motivation best. Under the pressures of federal reform, the only way to get it done is to "reinvent." "Ancient welfare management systems can't attract the talent you need and your ability to put something up—to design the mechanics for fast change— requires that you go around the constraints imposed by the civil service system." Further, given the changes in expectations for work among clients, welfare reform has resulted in both huge increases in resources for these services and "dynamic relationships with individuals that have altered the context and the opportunities for change."[22]

The need for speed made the logic simple. The administration of Mayor Rudolph Giuliani was already contracting in lots of areas, and social services, child welfare, and employment had been contracted out for decades. Welfare to work fit nicely into the city's strategy. Little would be lost by turning to private vendors, since the advantage of institutional memory in a system undergoing transformation seems to be limited. According to George Leutermann of MAXIMUS (instrumental in assisting the city's reform), "Thirty years of welfare knowledge is down the wastebasket with all of the changes that have occurred. Programs have changed so radically that the program history housed in welfare departments is obsolete; and with increasing reliance on contractors to shape new efforts, internal governmental capacity and expertise has been drained."[23]

Contracting provides increased capacity, opportunities to draw on new sources of talent, and means to circumvent the constraints on reengineering that recalcitrant civil service systems impose. But it also provides an opportunity to harness market forces to provide services "faster, cheaper, better."[24] In three of the four sites studied, contractors had economic incentives to provide required services more cheaply, since the structure of their performance-based contracts rewarded outcomes, and all stand to gain if a client is placed sooner, eschewing the longer, more expensive services.[25] Even in Houston, where contracts pay costs up to a maximum, pressures to reduce cost were apparent. Clients in an informal focus group experienced cost-cutting behavior firsthand, complaining about contractors of career centers who sought to lower staff-client ratios because of the need to keep costs in line with contracted budgets.[26] In other sites, public officials argue, performance-based contracts create incentives to provide stable, well-paid jobs for clients, since contractors receive increased payments per placement after a client can be certified to have been 60, 90, or 120 days on the job.[27] But critics in all sites have argued that this need to base service decisions on cost induces fewer services and services of reduced quality, and it encourages contractors to "cream" clients who are easier to place in preference to those who are harder (and more expensive) to serve. This was clearly the case in New York at the outset. Indeed, since the bulk of payments accrue at placement, contractors may determine that the economics favor getting clients into *any* job regardless of their longer-term success.

Early indications favor the critics, but performance data are hard to interpret. In Milwaukee the benchmarks are so low and contractors report they can all manipulate the reporting system known as CARES in such a way that distinctions between them are relatively meaningless. Virtually all contractors I interviewed in Milwaukee agreed. Dick Buschmann, the administrator for the Financial Assistance Division for the Milwaukee County Department of Human Services, identified performance standards as strong but subject to manipulation. He confirmed that the benchmarks are too low, that the methods of calculation and levels reported are problematic.[28] In contrast, analysis of comparative contractor performance in eight sites visited by the GAO researchers—Texas (Austin and Houston), California (Los Angeles and San Diego), Florida (Miami-Dade and Palm Beach), New York City, and Milwaukee—found that few met expected levels of performance in the areas of work participation, job placement, and job retention. Only Milwaukee and Palm Beach were found to have met expected performance levels. Profit or nonprofit status could not explain differences in contractor performance overall.[29]

Public officials are beginning to rethink the structure of and incentives in current contracts. In New York, for example, where implementation took longer than expected, a one-month snapshot of current average placement rates for all TANF clients referred to and seen by ESP contractors hovers at 29 percent, with retention at 90 days averaging only 9 percent and only 3 percent at 180 days.[30] These data, too, are controversial, since the denominators of the percentage calculations include those clients who may be still eligible to meet various performance milestones. Further, they cannot account for potential clients whom contractors simply turn away because their characteristics make them hard and expensive to place. Even so, the performance data provide strong support for the contention that placement is the most important milestone for contractors. While the performance of individual contractors varies significantly, several senior agency administrators are questioning the relative emphasis of the payment system that places a more significant economic incentive on initial placement than it does on retention. Even so, most public officials interviewed in Milwaukee, New York, and San Diego emphasized the managerial, technological, and service innovations that were likely to be created as a result of the economic incentives.

Jurisdictions had considerable confidence in the market to improve performance. The results of a competitive contracting environment, however, are hard to interpret. Whether the difficulties derive from the measurement problems, the contractor's intentional manipulation, or perverse incentives induced by the structure of the contracts, research to date has not been able to explain adequately the variation in contractor performance within and between sites. While each jurisdiction expected that circumventing the bureaucracy and public service unions, applying more business-like practices, and encouraging competition through the bidding process would provide the economic incentives to perform, the results have been mixed in most places. For-profits were no more likely to perform than public or nonprofit competitors.[31] In Arizona, the state contracted with MAXIMUS to provide services to some portion of the caseload, while the state provided them to the other portion. The effort was designed to see whether contracting with a private firm in an environment competitive with the state program would improve performance. Recent findings revealed no significant differences between the performance of the public agency and MAXIMUS.[32] Whatever the expectations, performing in this environment is difficult, and multiple factors appear to affect the likelihood of success.

Load Shedding and Reducing Administrative Burdens

While welfare reform has created the motivation and opportunity to experiment with different service delivery systems, most jurisdictions have had some history of contracting for employment and training services from nonprofit and private vendors—especially (for nonwelfare clients) under the Department of Labor's JTPA programs. Many of these experiences have placed the public agency in the role of contract manager for a multitude of nonprofits, small community-based organizations, and, less often, for-profit providers. While the potential virtues of contracting may be obvious, rarely do public officials responsible for service provision discuss the managerial burdens and challenges of managing and ensuring the performance of a large number of vendors. These administrative activities are onerous, and public agencies often do not do a good job of ensuring accountability through well-designed reporting systems and contract-monitoring functions.[33]

New York, for example, has been notoriously poor at monitoring the hundreds of contracts it has historically had with nonprofits for providing employment and training services.[34] The system was plagued by payment delays, backlogs in accounting, and failure to adequately assess contractor performance through its expenditure-based payment system. The current effort, which has contracted out the assessment and placement and the employment training and job placement functions, resulted in a dramatic change in contract management, shifting all monitoring and payment functions out of the programs and into HRA's department of finance. Instead of managing hundreds of small contracts, HRA is left with sixteen multimillion-dollar contracts. Many of the new providers will depend on dozens of subcontractors to meet the demands of their service commitments, but now it will be *their* role to negotiate the terms of their contracts and to monitor and ensure reporting compliance from their subs. The result, from the city's point of view, is a vast load shedding of reporting and monitoring functions to contractors and a reduced contract management function for sixteen contracts rather than hundreds of individual contracts.

The city argues that its new management system has resulted in cost savings and shifts in the roles and responsibilities of scores of city employees. Instead of dozens of clerical functions devoted to verifying and documenting the expenses of contractors, a new on-line vendor reporting system, allowing for immediate recording of job placement and attainment of payment milestones, has facilitated payment. All paperwork and staff devoted to processing have been eliminated. This is expected to result in far fewer payment delays and bureaucratic hassles, which characterized the expenditure-based system. These system changes are very recent, and time will tell whether they properly balance vendor needs with appropriate oversight. Implementation of a new monitoring system recognizes that prime contractors will play the role of monitor in a new accountability system. Since the primes are responsible for the behavior of their subs and HRA has reduced almost all monitoring to the verification of placements and retention by quarterly audits of a sample of cases from each vendor, verification requirements will be reserved for vendors whose audits reveal discrepancies between reported and documented placements. This shift in contract management process greatly reduces the city's administrative burden, but it may also reduce accountability. As one administrator reported, "We don't really care about the behavior of the subs and we don't really want to know how well they are managed. Money drives a lot of what happens and the economic incentives drive what they do."[35]

Many of the historic contract monitoring functions involved considerable technical assistance on the programming end. Under the new contracts, city officials do not meet regularly with individual contractors, and they spend no time monitoring programmatic aspects of vendor performance. Indeed, the shift to performance-based contracts has made outcomes the exclusive basis for oversight. One city official revealed that HRA currently conducts no ongoing audits other than those planned in the future, which will represent a small sample of cases. Indeed, they maintain a very small auditing staff compared with the staff once allocated by the Department of Employment, which used to manage employment contracts for the hundreds of smaller contractors providing services under JTPA. All previous monitoring staff at HRA was connected to programs. Now any remaining staff members have been reassigned to payment and finance or other program services. Savings accrued in staff costs, but real savings have come through management efficiencies that are now possible under a new management information system. Efforts to calculate the staff savings are difficult, however. While lower-level, lower-paid staff supported the onerous paper-based systems necessary for the review of receipts, invoices, and other vendor submissions under an expenditure-based payment system, the current performance-based system requires more staff with database and computer skills. While the numbers are lower, their salaries are higher. On a cost-per-placement basis, however, local officials argue that savings of the current system are significant.

GAO's study of accountability for contracted TANF providers lends support for the concern about the adequacy of accountability and monitoring in jurisdictions where contracting to private and nonprofit vendors is extensive. A New York State comptroller's audit in 2000 reported by the GAO found that New York State counties had not devoted sufficient priority or resources to carrying out their TANF monitoring responsibilities effectively. In addition, they found that the state contracting agency did not have information systems adequate to monitor and report on work participation by TANF recipients. New York State program officials reported that contracting agencies in the state "continue to experience ongoing shortfalls in staff resources necessary to provide sufficient oversight of contractor performance." New York City was found to have data quality issues that complicated efforts to monitor effectively. HRA reported time-consuming reviews and reconciliations when data on its automated systems on job placement and retention differed from case file information, resulting in delays in payments to contractors reported to total several million dollars.[36]

While monitoring and accountability are important to protect clients and to ensure program integrity, too much oversight can induce perverse effects that undermine the goals of contracting. Ironically, while New York has moved away from close scrutiny of contractors' programmatic choices and reduced the potential burdens on prime contractors for immediate paper documentation of placements, San Diego has moved in the opposite direction. Official reports stress the potential learning about best practice that comes from a performance-based system with explicit outcomes, but all contractors in San Diego complained about the increasing scrutiny of variations in programmatic activities and increasing demands for documentation of all their activities. In contrast to New York, where new management information systems were applauded, there has been criticism about the county's performance reporting system, and there are increasing requirements for contractors to document every single billing. An official of MAXIMUS, a private contractor with contracts for two county regions, described his frustration with the need to provide twenty-four pieces of documentation to collect $33.[37]

Accountability Threats

The obvious potential benefits of restructuring are clear, even as the risks for accountability loom large. New York City has, in effect, relinquished much of its authority and responsibility for oversight to third parties when it selects its contractors. Similar behavior was reported in Milwaukee. Some jurisdictions serve as many as 50 percent of their clients through their subcontractors or community partners. Oversight of their behavior is necessary to avert potentially serious consequences for clients. While contracting out may appear to relieve local governments of costly and onerous contract management functions, the need for appropriate systems of oversight is ever greater to protect vulnerable populations. Where previously smaller contractors in New York were receiving contracts for tens of thousands or hundreds of thousands of dollars, the sixteen current contracts range from seven or eight million dollars (over three years) to as much as $84.8 million for Goodwill Industries, which won two contracts under New York City's negotiated acquisition process.[38] In contrast, San Diego may be squandering the potential innovations and cost savings of its system. Fear of placing too much responsibility for program decisions on the contractors has led to a program guide that mandates much of the sequence contractors must follow. Contractors complain about excessive rules, regulations, and documentation requirements that constrain their choices. Efforts to control contractor choices and programmatic design too closely, coupled with excessive, expensive, and burdensome documentation have increased contractor compliance but reduced their freedom to innovate.

Milwaukee's management of W-2 contracts was no better. The five contractors there were subject to minimal programmatic or financial monitoring, even though the state had contracted with the local Private Industry Council for oversight and had originally given them great authority. A senior county official in Milwaukee explained that since monitoring was ultimately controlled by the state, organizations never felt accountable to the Private Industry Council, and the state simply did not "allocate enough resources or have enough interest in accountability. They were only concerned about getting the caseload down."[39] Concerns about contractor behavior, however, ultimately resulted in an audit by the Wisconsin state legislature that revealed misuse of public funds not exposed previously by any existing systems of oversight. The audit revealed that even though contractors also were responsible for eligibility determination, they had failed to inform clients about entitlements and supportive services for which they were eligible. While failure to do so might have resulted in cost savings for the contractor, it compromised the well-being of clients and their likelihood of maintaining long-term employment. No systematic oversight ensured controls on contractor behavior. In response the state has "contracted back in," awarding county workers a $5 million contract to take over the initial needs assessments and referrals of clients seeking assistance to ensure that those clients are not denied available or needed services.[40] When contractors' economic interests compete with the public interest, the need for better oversight and monitoring is obvious.

In contracting out many of the welfare-to-work services and increasing the role of for-profit providers, public executives are attempting to increase service capacity quickly, to create competitive pressures to reduce costs and improve efficiency, and to reduce the administrative burdens on public agencies. The use of a few large contractors in each site creates a system of managed competition, not unlike that found in the health-care sector. Managing a few large contracts as the primes themselves manage the subs adapts a model increasingly used in government contracts for large capital projects.

In New York, for example, for large construction projects, the city contracts with a construction management firm that, for 10 percent of the contract, hires and monitors the subcontractors. However, rather than reducing the need for expertise and contract management functions in public agencies, this approach requires greater investment, since the stakes are higher. Kettl's investigations of contracting in many federal, state, and local governments identified the problem. "Perhaps more important than ensuring competition in any particular market, the government must maintain its capacity to manage its contracts. As government has turned to private contractors for more of its administrative and support services, worries about the ability to manage these contractors have multiplied. . . . The more government has contracted out its core functions, the more the government worsens its problems of capacity building."[41]

There is little evidence, however, that public officials in New York and elsewhere have improved their oversight or increased their personnel commitments to ensure that they perform these functions well. Indeed, it may take increased revelations of abuses to ensure that proper accountability functions are in place. Nevertheless, contracting agencies must learn to balance oversight with the freedom to innovate in managing contracts. San Diego has hamstrung its providers with excessive and dysfunctional regulations.[42] Neither New York nor San Diego will exploit the potential that contracting provides.[43]

Management Improvements?

The zeal with which public officials are embracing the market varies. Most see the virtues of competition and the comparative advantages that for-profits add to the mix. First Deputy Commissioner Mark Hoover of New York's HRA singled out the virtues of a process neither dictated nor driven by government: "Investment decisions are made by the contractor, not government." Firms get paid and make a profit only after meeting critical milestones. To reduce the incentives for minimizing services to clients to increase potential profits under some contracts, profits are capped, as they are in Milwaukee.[44] As Commissioner Hoover pointed out: best of all, for-profits pay taxes.

Nevertheless, a number of observers view the changes less as a victory for the market and more as experiments from which to learn. In an environment of performance-based contracts, comparative data will be available to assess each of the contractors for a subsequent round of bidding. Further, the online reporting system to which each vendor has access provides an ongoing ranking of all performance outcomes, so firms can see how well they are doing in relationship to the other vendors. This access to comparative performance data has induced greater competition among providers. Joan Zinser in San Diego described the county's motivation for its managed competition design: "We wanted to see who could do it best, so that when we hit the hardest to serve we have the data."[45] While not all sites expressed the same level of enthusiasm for the virtues of the market, all valued the benefits of competition that the inclusion of for-profit entities brought.

In New York, however, public officials have taken a strong ideologically based position and were able to articulate a broader, more philosophical justification for their approach. First Deputy Commissioner Mark Hoover argued, "Government is best at setting desired outcomes, designing policies, and overseeing and supervising their implementation. Government is not great at operational activities or service delivery; there are simply too many processes and inefficiencies in government. Contracting is better, cheaper, and more flexible. You can add or contract as needed. While government requires equal access, and responsiveness to other values that society imposes on it, government *itself* has problems ensuring access and accountability. Government simply cannot do these things efficiently. Good management works better outside."[46] Other sites, less ideologically driven, are more pragmatic. They have relied on more traditional forces—such as political pressure and familiarity—to support the redesign of their systems and their selection of vendors, which often favored established and popular nonprofits.

Legal Challenges

Outsourcing appeared an ideal way to circumvent many of the bureaucratic obstacles to reengineering. Efforts, however, to circumvent constraints imposed by public employee contracts may be more difficult to achieve than most public officials anticipated. San Diego, in its efforts to move quickly to meet strict time constraints to implement its CalWORKs (California Work Opportunity and Responsibility to Kids) program (five and a half months from enactment to implementation), undertook its contracting process without conducting state-mandated "efficiency and economy analyses" required by the county charter whenever discretionary functions are to be performed by any vendor other than county employees. Further, a recent judgment in a suit brought by the San Diego County Service Employees International Union dealt additionally with whether these services under the county charter could be provided by private vendors at all, even if such a study were conducted. Under the leadership of Larry Prior, then the county's chief administrative officer, contracting out case management in San Diego to private and nonprofit vendors constituted but one part of a multipronged effort to introduce competition-based reform in multiple service delivery areas to bring greater levels of cost savings, performance, and efficiency.[47] San Diego County has appealed the court's ruling, which found in favor of the county employees, and current contracts will continue for the two years estimated for the appeals process to be completed. During that time the county is committed to undertaking the economy and efficiency study required.

Such difficulties are not unique to San Diego. In 1996 Texas attempted to go beyond all current efforts and privatize the whole of its welfare system—including income and eligibility determination—through the Texas Integrated Enrollment Services (TIES) program. As in San Diego, however, the local unions protested, and eventually President Clinton disallowed the broad use of private companies to determine eligibility for entitlement programs. New York, too, has had $104 million in contracts to MAXIMUS disallowed by the courts on the grounds of fraud in the bidding process. The MAXIMUS decision was reversed on appeal, but the contracts were reinstated, two years after they were originally granted, and for much reduced amounts and functions.[48] When the contracts expired, they were allowed to lapse.

Controversy and legal challenges threaten both the speed and the effectiveness sought by using private firms. Political opponents of all stripes have challenged the contracting process and the wisdom of relying on private for-profit firms at all. Their effectiveness in launching a credible attack can be witnessed by the increasing reluctance of firms to bid in areas with inhospitable political environments whatever the possible benefits. Representatives of MAXIMUS in all the sites studied have pointed to the high costs of defending against presumptions of ethical or financial lapses that attend public perceptions of for-profit firms. One representative even suggested that a strategy to avoid the costly scrutiny and political hazards might be to act as a subcontractor under a nonprofit prime. As mounting legal and administrative costs offset anticipated savings, some jurisdictions contemplating large-scale contracting may be forced to rethink their strategies.

A recent dispute in Florida is typical. Lockheed Martin IMS had the sole-source contract after 1999 in Florida's Pinellas County to provide job placement and training services. The twenty-month, $15 million contract was terminated by the company with accusations that the county had breached its contract and owed IMS more than a million dollars. County officials argue that Lockheed Martin IMS had performed badly in Pinellas compared with other Florida counties, and the disputed amounts are attributed in part to poor record-keeping.[49] IMS, sold recently to ACS State and Local Solutions, Inc., has filed suit against the county, beginning a process that will be costly for both the county and ACS. Contractual disputes of this sort are costly for both sides and often disrupt client services and threaten public efforts to meet federal requirements. They often discourage local officials from contracting and undermine contractors' willingness to compete in certain markets.

Conclusion

Whatever the promise of contracting, the early experience of each of the jurisdictions studied is clearly mixed. Initial optimism about market-driven arrangements was high, but start-up problems persist. As each jurisdiction moves to its next round of contracts, most of the elements of the contracting system are under review. Experience with variable performance on both placement and retention may necessitate changes in the design and economic incentives of contracts, which will require ongoing evaluation of the mix of contractors, the character of monitoring, and the expenditures allocated per client. These changes may respond to the realities of current efforts, which were forged under serious time constraints and with little experience, especially in the design of contracts and systems to manage them.

While New York developed state-of-the-art management information systems to replace pencil-and-paper processing, San Diego increased its documentation requirements, creating heavy burdens on contractors. Both approaches will likely require some adjustments in future contracts as public officials balance efforts to reduce administrative costs and oversight. Subsequent contracts will not be designed with the same pressure and speed that accompanied initial contracts responding hastily to the new TANF mandates. However, considerable uncertainty exists about the challenges states will face as they adjust their delivery systems in subsequent rounds of contracts. State and local decisionmakers must adapt their contracts facing an uncertain economy, a growing preponderance of caseloads with increasing barriers to employment, and the increased demands and reduced federal allocations that may accompany the reauthorization legislation currently under debate. Further, they must do so when many experienced public officials are leaving government to serve the growing private sector in this industry.

No site I studied experienced a smooth transition to contracting. Experiential learning is likely to improve performance over time if managers with contract expertise can be retained. It seems clear that contract management and the design of performance-based contracts are as much art as science, and experience matters. Even so, no public official interviewed for this study had any serious questions about the value or role that contracting would play in long-term planning. Indeed, early implementation experiences have highlighted areas for improvement and concern, but revealed little meaningful controversy or serious political activity that might threaten the continued commitment to market-driven arrangements or the inclusion of for-profit firms.

CHAPTER FOUR

Nonprofits: Meeting New Challenges

These have been turbulent times for nonprofits. Increased competition with the private sector has exacerbated sweeping changes that are influencing what nonprofits do, how they do it, and how successful they are. The past two decades have witnessed phenomenal growth in the nonprofit sector, even while critics and expert observers have sounded the alarms. The future of the sector is under continual scrutiny, but our judgments about its condition depend on whether we see the glass as half empty or half full. Paul Light has identified the reform movement that has put significant pressure on nonprofits to improve, and many organizations are feeling the squeeze from all sides. Even so, Light reminds us that in many respects, the sector has grown significantly in the dollars it receives from contributors and government, in the size and professionalism of its work force, and in the career aspirations of a new generation whose members increasingly see the nonprofit sector as their destination.[1] Nevertheless, the sector is facing increasing pressures to demonstrate its effectiveness. Increasingly nonprofits are being asked to justify their competence and relevance.

Nonprofits in the welfare-to-work industry face the same pressures as those operating in other areas. But in many respects, they are in a better position to make the case for their continuing importance as players in a restructured delivery system. Most have social missions that commit them to improving the well-being of disadvantaged populations, and many have been doing this work for a long time.[2] Embedded in their communities, many community-based nonprofits possess cultural competence and have preexisting connections to the target populations they serve. Further, they are linked to the local resources and institutions that are capable of providing support for clients with special needs. Even so, they face challenging times. Pressures to demonstrate performance in program outcomes, fiscal and organizational management, and efficiency have been mounting from a more sophisticated donor base, funding institutions, boards of directors, professionalized staff, and government; and reform movements are besetting the sector.[3]

Government contracts and funding represent an ever-increasing proportion of nonprofits' income. As early as 1982, 56 percent of all social services and 48 percent of all employment and training services financed by government were delivered by nonprofits.[4] Between 1992 and 1998, public support for employment and training nonprofits increased by 44 percent. [5] Government funds continue to compose a high proportion of income for social service organizations. While recent data on sources of funding for nonprofit employment and training providers alone are hard to find, 1997 data on the proportion of revenues that nonprofit social services organizations receive from government sources put the figure in excess of 52 percent.[6] This figure probably underestimates the percentage among employment and training providers where nonprofits still provide the bulk of services to state and local governments and for whom government historically was the single largest source of funding.

While the increasing reliance of state and local governments on nonprofits to deliver social services has resulted in significant growth, it has also made the survival of these organizations vulnerable to changes in government expenditures and policies. A study that analyzed the impact of federal welfare waivers on human services nonprofits in the fifty-three largest metropolitan areas found that 26 percent failed from 1992 to 1996.[7] Another study of 13,500 nonprofits most likely to be affected by welfare reform found that of the 83 percent that were providing core services (including employment-related services), revenue was growing, but for a majority, expenditures were growing at a faster rate. Only 41 percent of these nonprofits had positive net balances for the two years of the study.[8] These data highlight nonprofits' vulnerability to policy and funding changes. Some are better capitalized and managed.[9] Others have more diverse funding streams, allowing them greater resiliency and adaptability to changing policy demands and economic fluctuations. Nonprofits that fail are quickly replaced by new entrants—at a rate of three new human-service providers for each one that fails.[10] What seems clear, however, is that greater competition, increasing dependence on government, and changing standards and expectations for nonprofit performance pose serious challenges for the future.

Fiscal, economic, and effectiveness crises represent significant ongoing challenges for nonprofit institutions. However, Lester Salamon has dubbed the more fundamental crisis in the nonprofit sector one of legitimacy.[11] A more fundamental moral and political challenge, the legitimacy crisis Salamon identifies describes the problem facing the sector as one that questions its continued raison d'être. Wedded to a nineteenth-century image of charity and altruism, public support for nonprofits in the wake of their commercialization, public partnerships, and professionalization appears to be on the decline.

> The nonprofit sector is thus being hoisted on its own mythology. Having failed to make clear to the American public what its role should be in a mature mixed economy, the sector has been thrown on the defensive by revelations that it is not operating the way its mythology would suggest. A massive gap has thus opened between the modern reality of a sector intimately involved with government and moving into commercialization in the wake of government cutbacks, and the popular image of a set of community based institutions mobilizing purely voluntary energies to assist those in need.[12]

Nonprofits engaged in welfare-to-work contracting, both large institutions and smaller CBOs, are indeed obliged to reexamine their missions, governance, and ways of operating, especially in a competitive, performance-based service environment. Success requires that they compare themselves with private for-profit firms and elevate market values in their decisions about what challenges to pursue and how to pursue them. As nonprofits are in transition in this environment, they are more like the "shadow state." They are ever in conflict about the autonomy they can maintain and the participatory or democratic objectives they can pursue. "As the sector struggles to maintain itself and develop, it faces a difficult dilemma: to rely increasingly on opportunities linked to state privatization initiatives (and, hence, subject itself to increasing state control) or to maintain independence of organizational purpose but face a continuing struggle for survival and resources. Either way, the sector's survival remains at risk."[13]

Nonprofits in the four sites studied are experiencing considerable stress in making the shifts necessary to become more business-like in organizational design, management, staffing, and culture when they compete for welfare-to-work contracts. The degree of difficulty experienced varies considerably among organizations of different size, experience, sophistication, and philosophy. However, as figure 3-1 illustrated, the pressure exerted by private-sector competitors in all the sites is significant; and all the nonprofits understand the substantial challenges they face. The sections that follow describe the differences in their motivations for competing for contracts and the differential effects of their recent adjustments. Some are successfully adapting but in danger of "losing their souls"; others are struggling to develop the capacity to compete; and still others face more immediate threats to their survival.

Playing the Game; Keeping Your Soul

Nonprofits that succeeded in the bidding process were generally experienced service providers with a history of contracting to government and with missions focused on serving disadvantaged populations. Many, but not all, had provided case management, employability assessment, and job placement and/or training services under a wide range of government funding streams and/or private philanthropic resources. Many had some degree of skepticism about the future under a competitive contract process with for-profit organizations. Most, however, were motivated to participate by a commitment to serve low-income populations consistent with their missions.

Most of the nonprofit executives I interviewed held the view that the "world is changing." As Nancy Liu of the Chinese Community Center in Houston put it, "If you are behind the wagon, then you are behind the wagon no matter what. It doesn't matter what kind of heart that you have. There is just no money for you to have a good heart and not see what the bottom line is."[14] While the role of nonprofit providers in the design of new delivery systems and contracts varied, with some long-term providers expressing dismay about the lack of consultation in the system redesign process, all felt that, given their experience and missions, they should have a role in a redesigned system. One nonprofit executive, Sister Raymonda DuVall, executive director of Catholic Charities in San Diego, described the motivation in these terms: "We bid because we didn't trust the city to deal fairly with the poor. We wanted to have a voice at the table. The for-profits have no mission or commitment toward the poor. We thought, once they get a foothold, the nonprofits would be out of business."[15] In a presentation before a group of welfare administrators from around the country, Sister DuVall described the motivation further as emanating directly from their mission and because the federal legislation compelled them to embrace "a unique opportunity to do it right."[16]

In Houston, the Community Services branch of the local AFL-CIO bid for a contract and won. Capitulating to the realities of prevailing policy, rather than relinquish their role, they chose to compete in an arena consistently under attack by labor unions across the nation. The AFL-CIO director, Richard Shaw, explained the situation in terms similar to those of Sister DuVall, that if that were the fate of the state, labor could not sit out and lose its opportunity to be part of it.[17]

The nonprofit response to the changing environment is clearly a marriage of pragmatism and social mission. There was the recognition that this was the only game in town, a game where the players were eligible for far more resources than most had ever had in a single contract (see figure 4-1). This judgment was balanced by a view expressed by most of those we spoke to: that this was the business that they were in, and they had a mission-driven belief that they could do it better. Amalia Betanzos, president of Wildcat Service Corporation, with a $54.7 million contract in New York, was particularly enthusiastic about their ability to perform under a performance-based contract and eager to demonstrate her group's superiority as a provider. "We have always exceeded our benchmarks, so we are pleased with performance-based contracts. We want to get paid for our results and will do well under this system. If you are good, competition is useful—compared with for-profits, our motivations are different. This is our business—this is their opportunity."[18]

Many even claimed they welcomed the competition from the private sector because they found the competitive pressures made them better, but that the financial structure of their operations, and their long experience in the community, dealing with disadvantaged clients and employers, gave them a comparative advantage. Most of the nonprofits I interviewed—and the majority of the current nonprofit contractors who won bids in the latest round—were relatively well capitalized, in the business a long time, and felt: "We know exactly what we are (compared with the new entrants into the system)."[19] Even so, asset levels, even for large

Figure 4-1. *Nonprofit Income and Assets (2000) Compared with Contract Amount (2001)*

Millions of dollars

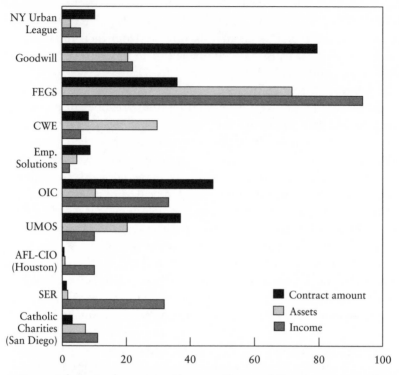

Source: Information from www.guidestar.org. Ten out of thirteen contract providers are included for which data were available.

Note: Goodwill = Goodwill Industries (New York); FEGS = Federal Employment and Guidance Services (New York); CWE = Consortium for Worker Education (New York); Emp. Solutions = Employment Solutions (Milwaukee); OIC = Opportunities Industrialization Center of Greater Milwaukee; UMOS = United Migrant Opportunities Services (Milwaukee); SER = SER-Jobs for Progress (Houston).

nonprofits, are often rather low in comparison with the size of contracts they are taking (see figure 4-1 and appendix A).

Goodwill Industries of New York, for example, is a large, well-established player nationally and in the New York provider community, in business for more than eighty years. Its business is work preparation. Goodwill Industries runs a thrift-shop business that recycles, repairs, and cleans used items like clothing and furniture to be sold in its retail shops across the city. These businesses train the disabled, low-income, and youth for private-sector employment. CEO Rex Davidson identified Goodwill's advantages over its competitors for welfare-to-work (both for-profit and nonprofits) in philosophy and operations. Having its own business provides Goodwill with independence as a place for on-the-job training. Its multiple funding sources—from its business activities and philanthropy—reduce its dependence on government. "We have an efficient model to produce programs and service: we use for-profit management techniques and sophisticated systems of financial management which result in audits which always pass scrutiny. We run businesses and embrace business-oriented management techniques. We are reliable and our results are predictable. We have the lowest overhead in the country and can fund our operations upfront through high capitalization. We're here and we'll be here when the money dries up." Further, Goodwill can place clients in employment in their own industry. "We believe in the power of work. If you don't work you can't learn to work. The dignity of employment, you can't replace that!"[20]

Given its scale, reputation, experience, and business-oriented values (and relationships with employers), Goodwill would appear an ideal contractor for the city. Indeed, it holds two of the largest contracts in New York City's reengineered welfare delivery system. Even so, the new mega-contracts have represented significant challenges. At a combined $84 million for the two contracts over three years,[21] the new contract dollars represent more than twice as much as their current asset base, an amount that makes them highly vulnerable to the city's funding and policy shifts. Further, though Davidson argued, "Competition is good. It makes us better. As long as it's not the be all and end all," Goodwill's current performance places it below average among the other contractors in the percentage of clients placed and in last place for retention. This is the case despite its articulated commitment to client follow-up on the job and its subcontracts with a large number of CBOs that provide specialized services in their communities.[22] Whether their performance problems stem from the scale of their operations, the performance of their subcontractors, or the city's generally acknowledged difficulties in referring an adequate number of assessed clients, it is clear that even highly capable and experienced providers are having difficulties in this environment.

The big dilemma for the large stable nonprofits is whether they will compromise their missions of putting the client first and tailoring their services to the individual needs of the client. Performance-based contracts and current payment levels favor rapid placement of clients and few specialized services that must be paid for out of the fixed maximum payments for which contractors are eligible. Many of the nonprofit leaders interviewed bemoan the structure and incentives of the contracts themselves. The Women's Housing and Economic Development Corporation (WHEDCO) became a partner with America Works and a subcontractor to Wildcat Service Corporation in the reengineered service delivery system in New York—unable to compete alone for a prime contract. WHEDCO's president, Nancy Biberman, described the problem this way:

> The ESP program and contracts were never intended to result in viable jobs for welfare recipients. The rapid reduction of the welfare caseload was the public policy mandate out of which the ESP program was created. The ESP contracts were children of short-sighted social policy and privatization ideology, which have proven both costly and inappropriate in the human services sector. . . . The contracts were structured to provide financial incentives for "rapid labor market attachment" (the expressly stated goal of HRA commissioner Jason Turner). Consequently, at best they provided quick job placements and woefully unsatisfactory job retention outcomes. The policy has proven egregiously myopic. The current labor market contraction has left those with the poorest skills most vulnerable to layoffs. Had the ESP contracts been structured to enable participants to develop marketable skills before diving into low-wage dead-end jobs, perhaps long-term job retention could have been achieved. But the payment milestones in these "performance-based" contracts, coupled with WEP, forced even the most mission-driven providers into unconscionable work.[23]

Only in Houston, where contractors are paid on a cost-reimbursement basis for specified services up to a maximum, is there an incentive to vary the service package. Yet even there concerns have been raised about contractors' choosing the easiest to serve to ensure higher success rates. The diversified funding streams that characterize many of the nonprofits, but none of the for-profits (like foundation and private fundraising sources), can allow for cross subsidy and cost-sharing among different programs. In this way they can pay for services clients may need but that current contract amounts do not accommodate. Obviously the economic incentives built into these contracts go in the opposite direction and pose a dilemma for mission-driven nonprofits.

A recent development in Wisconsin following a state legislative audit in Milwaukee provides additional support for concerns about the perverse effects—even for mission driven nonprofits—of the economic incentive central to the contract design.[24] Milwaukee's contracts are comprehensive and include eligibility determination in addition to job readiness and placement services.[25] The Milwaukee W-2 Advisory Panel recommended changes in the Milwaukee program in response to revelations of state audits that relatively few clients were advised by contracting agencies about a range of available services for which they were eligible. Further, the audits confirmed that few had adequate assessment of their needs, had been lifted out of poverty, or had been placed in more intensive education and training programs that might have led to self-supporting jobs. The audits implied that contract agencies simply did not offer services if clients did not request them. The money saved by not offering them, presumably, represented cost savings to the contractors and contributed to their profits.

In response, under a newly funded arrangement, the state has allocated $5 million for a contract for county workers to assume the role at the "front door," undertaking client assessments and informing them of the services for which they are eligible—including job training and food stamps. Then they will be referred to appropriate W-2 agencies. These changes are designed to ensure that clients will be aware of their entitlements and the supportive services available. The need for changes like these, however, illustrates the potential conflicts between the cost-saving (profit-maximizing) incentives inherent in performance-based contracts and serving clients' interests. The legislative audit uncovered evidence of the potentially serious consequences of the economic incentives inherent in contract design in the absence of systems to ensure appropriate monitoring and accountability. These were dangers generally thought to exist when for-profit firms provide the services. Most observers thought the values of nonprofits and their missions would ensure against contractual abuses. However, both were found to have denied clients critical access to information about their eligibility for additional services and program resources. Whether these oversights were necessary to meet contract demands, nonprofits may be forced to capitulate to market pressures, compromising their values to remain competitive with for-profits.

Living by Their Wits

Large stable nonprofits with large and diversified funding streams appear relatively secure. In many ways they resemble their for-profit

competitors more than they do their leaner, less business-oriented counterparts among nonprofit—especially CBO—providers.[26] However,
many nonprofits in the employment and training business are facing an
insecure future in a changing environment. Some of the medium-sized
and smaller organizations are regrouping, shifting their focus, and looking for alternative sources of both government and private funding.
These efforts to survive combine a search for new dollars, development
of new areas of program growth, investments in improved management
to achieve cost savings, and some efforts to embrace private market
techniques. Some nonprofits have developed for-profit subsidiaries to
realize some of the benefits that accrue to the for-profit providers.
Catholic Charities in San Diego was typical. It underwent a significant
management reorganization, including the development of a more professionalized set of management and personnel systems and introduction
of a new generation of technological and information systems, in order
to be competitive and manage its recent contracts with the county. Similarly, Houston Works has modernized to such a degree that it has been
described as having become the leading edge in business technology—
comparable to industry leaders like the for-profit Lockheed Martin IMS.

A particularly innovative effort characterized one of the smaller nonprofits that won a $7.4 million contract in New York. Seedco, a highly
respected medium-sized nonprofit with areas of investment that include
community and economic development, work force development, and
housing, has built a collaborative with fifteen CBOs to provide technical
assistance while helping to provide employment training and job placement to TANF recipients under the New York City contract. Organized
as a subsidiary to the nonprofit Seedco, the Non-Profit Assistance Corporation (N-PAC) has structured a limited liability corporation (LLC)
named EarnFair to take advantage of a range of private-sector incentives
such as an ability to use allowable tax credits as an eligible employer of
welfare recipients. As an LLC, EarnFair can operate as a temporary
employment agency and syndicate these tax credits using the additional
resources from their sale to subsidize increased and more intensive services to the clients it serves. Further, the N-PAC subsidiary runs the welfare-to-work program using the collaboration of CBOs and generates
additional funding from a diverse set of resources, including philanthropic and other public funds.

Seedco's president, Bill Grinker, an innovator in human services and
former HRA commissioner himself, described the vision:

We view ourselves as a management service entity. The key service provision is provided through CBOs. Our interest is in providing information systems, capacity, financial assistance, and technical, programmatic types of supports. While theoretically we are the prime contractor, we view the CBOs as "partners" rather than subs. Even so, these CBOs would most likely be closed out of these contracts had they not been able to come under the umbrella of a well-managed, fiscally sound prime.[27]

In actuality, N-PAC functions as a conduit for resources and information, "pooling together public and private grants and funds that it passes on to the subcontractor. As a result, N-PAC has to rely on job placements for only 50 percent of its funding, freeing up considerable resources to invest in longer-term training."[28] Perhaps most important, Seedco manages the financial risk for the CBOs by basing its payments only partially on performance and the rest on a line-item, cost basis. The transparency with which each partner shares the performance data of the other partners creates pressure on each to be accountable.

The $7.4 million contract from the city represents only 20 percent of the resources N-PAC is allocating to this effort. The rest comes from the syndicated tax credits and other partners, such as the United Way, the New York Community Trust, and Local Initiatives Support Corporation (LISC), a community development intermediary. These resources allow innovative programmatic designs that go well beyond what other competitors could provide, most specifically the for-profits. Indeed, the EarnFair model provides post-placement support services and case management for participants for two years. It operates as a temp agency, but provides supervision of workers after placement with a private employer and provides additional supports on the job, including transitional services, fringe packages, counseling, and financing. Total wage packages are assembled that include the value of the Earned Income Tax Credit (EITC).

The EarnFair Model is a good example of Seedco's high standards for all our products. The program design itself embodies some of the best thinking in the welfare-to-work field about effective interventions. We also have in place a plan for long-term financing. We're not looking for financing that consists of one big government contract, but for diverse revenue streams. Having seen nonprofits struggle when government contracts are cut or living hand to mouth year after year, it's exciting to me to be working on economically sustainable financing for social purposes.[29]

Another innovative partnership developed in order to bid for a contract in Milwaukee. Simpler in concept, the YWCA partnered with CNR Health and the Kaiser Group to form a limited liability corporation in Milwaukee's District 1. In this arrangement, the YWCA became the managing partner of YW-WORKS, controlling day-to-day operations, while Kaiser and CNR Health provided many of the management systems and technological supports.[30] The Y had "a lot to bring to the table" since it had been involved throughout its history since the 1920s in employment and training—especially nontraditional training for women, Rita Rinner, YW-Works COO, reported. When the first RFPs were released in Milwaukee for W-2, "We wanted other expertise. We felt it was too risky to go it alone. CNR was a software developer, and we worried about the size of the budget and the risk of debt from a capitated payment if we failed. We needed technology, an MIS system, and help with reporting systems—partners could help."[31]

Partnerships such as these allow nonprofits to capture the benefits of private-sector capital, efficiencies, and management expertise while operating in a manner consistent with their missions. Private-sector partners helped to underwrite the risk, hire staff, and build needed infrastructure. In the second round of Milwaukee contracts, however, YW-Works dissolved the relationship and bid alone. Whatever the initial advantages, cultural differences plagued their relationships—differences in style and values. After they felt confident of their own management and technological capacity, they were less dependent on the partnership. Their private partners lost some interest as well. They found the environment and the bias against for-profits inhospitable. The political heat and the controversy that typically accompany the entrance of for-profit providers in a service area historically dominated by government and nonprofits made the arrangement uncomfortable. County providers around the state "have the view that private agencies can't be responsible with public funds."[32] However, the arrangement served the short-term transitional needs of the Y, helping it set up for an independent operation with the capacity to go it alone.

Innovative partnerships served some nonprofits well, but many other traditional employment and training providers were scrambling to stay in business. Many viewed the payment levels and schedules as unrealistically low under the contracts. A smaller contractor in New York who was unable to bid directly for any of the contracts and became a subcontractor for two of the primes (one for-profit and one nonprofit) described the situation: "Our reimbursement as a sub won't cover our costs. We'll have to fund raise to cover costs. . . . But our key advantage is our diversified funding. We see government contracts as defraying costs, not covering them."[33] This sentiment was repeated in Houston: "If you [as a local CBO] rely totally on government money, it is almost impossible for you to survive."[34] The contracts provide no incentive for long-term investment. For the subs, who must relinquish overhead to the prime, current payment schedules may pay only a fraction of the true costs of serving a disadvantaged client. But accepting these subcontracts allows for financial piggybacking and economies of scale for multiple-program cost sharing.

For small nonprofits, whose financial solvency depends on their performance, reasonable numbers, quality referrals, and timely payment for performance (which depends on the administrative performance of both the county or city and the prime), the financial risks are clearly high. A generalized concern among all the nonprofits interviewed that were acting as subcontractors was a fear about referrals. They feared, first, that the city or county would not refer sufficient numbers of eligible clients in a timely fashion to the prime to support the heavy investment in program operations. Even worse, they feared that the primes might "cream" the most job-ready clients for themselves and refer out the most difficult—and costly—to place, those with multiple barriers to employment.

Diane Baillargeon, Seedco vice president, who is familiar with the plight of many CBOs, reported: "There are already nonprofits, mostly small, relatively low capacity community-based organizations who have gotten out of the business . . . and I know personally of a number of organizations that simply have said we can't compete in this business any longer and they have gotten out of it. Now, most of them are multiservice, social service, community-based, community centers, and they are still operating their domestic violence program, and their homeless shelter, and all of that, but they are no longer in the workforce business. And I think that's a loss."[35]

In Houston, the system is designed to provide "customer choice."[36] No contract is signed with subcontractors and CBOs. Instead, training providers are chosen by the clients themselves after being counseled and given provider information by contractors at career centers. This system wreaks havoc on providers' planning processes, since they are unable to anticipate the demand for their services and the staffing those services might require. Further, in order to attract and keep clients, they must provide considerable information and do aggressive marketing. These are investments that they have no assurances will be recouped, nor for which many nonprofits have much expertise. Often CBOs invest considerable resources in initial recruiting and training before they refer clients to career centers to be certified, hoping they will return for more intensive services. These up-front investments are difficult for smaller nonprofits and CBOs to finance themselves. This process, known as reverse referrals, was seen as extremely costly for the nonprofits, but also necessary to ensure that even some initial contacts would return to their organizations. If they fail to find and attract a sufficient number of clients, given the tremendous number of choices clients have (more than 6,000 qualified providers, at last count), thousands of historic nonprofit providers may be forced to close their doors, seek new funding streams, or refocus their efforts on new service areas.[37]

The current strategy of the municipalities in this study has been to find a few experienced contractors with good track records and sufficient technological and managerial expertise to provide the services and information necessary to ensure full participation and job placement of all eligible clients. Federal mandates and the terms of performance-based contracts require information systems to track and verify the progress of all clients in the system, and these demands often require sophisticated technology and management systems. Many of the for-profit providers have considerable advantages in providing these systems. Indeed, Seedco used the philanthropic resources it raised for its innovative effort to purchase MIS software from a subsidiary of MAXIMUS—allowing them the same kind of capacity for its CBO partners as the for-profit firms. However, the development of these systems is expensive, even if they are bought "off the shelf," and few small organizations have the resources for such investments.

In New York and Milwaukee nonprofit providers have had a long history and good records of providing employment and training services, yet many lack the necessary technological and managerial systems to manage performance-based contracts. Further, because the timing of payments depends on performance in Milwaukee, New York, and San

Diego and on systems to verify placements, considerable up-front capital is necessary to undertake these contracts. The for-profits have considerable advantages over the nonprofits in assuming the risks. They have greater capacity to sustain operations in anticipation of future payment streams, since they have access to investment capital. Only a fraction of the nonprofits historically operating in the employment and training business have the ability to stay the course while they wait for payment. So serious was the threat to contractors in New York that the city was forced to provide some up-front working capital to sustain the start-up cost of its large TANF contracts.

Clearly the availability of working capital, more likely to characterize the larger for-profit companies, is a key factor in how competitive nonprofit providers can be over time. As Richard Shaw of the Houston AFL-CIO concluded, "First you have to have the money to spend the money, which is a real problem for small companies."[38] Further, how well capitalized an organization needs to be to remain solvent in this environment depends in large part on the competence and efficiency of the public agency responsible for reviewing and authorizing payments. Timely and accurate payments and an adequate flow of client referrals to providers depend on the management systems and capability of public agencies, and their recent track record is not encouraging.[39] Even large well-managed nonprofits such as Goodwill and Wildcat worried about the city's capacity to ensure that these functions were well managed.

New York's HRA has been notoriously poor at paying its vendors in a timely manner.[40] So problematic has been this lack of capacity that the city has had to advance most of the contractors payments of up to three months to keep them afloat. Further, the city is about to launch a new computerized system to receive vendor placements, make referrals, and speed up the process of calculating and verifying payments. While the system promises to improve on its speed of payments, current vendors still complain about the backlog and the critical amounts they are owed. This falls particularly heavily on subcontractors, whose payments flow from the city to the prime and then on to them. A representative of WHEDCO, a subcontractor for two large primes, described the problem:

One of the most debilitating footnotes to this story involves untimely payments of the paltry funds available under these contracts. At any given time, our organization awaited at least $100,000 in "receivables" from prime contractors. We had no recourse to the city, although we tried. Indeed, when we learned that a prime contractor had already been paid by the city for the work we had done, the city officials told us that we should *sue* the prime for payment![41]

The concern over cities' ability to refer clients resonates around the country. Holly Payne of MAXIMUS reported in an interview, "It is the biggest issue we face. It really is like pulling teeth trying to get these clients out of the system. The bureaucracy is horrible. For example, in Philadelphia there are 65,000 clients on welfare. MAXIMUS had a contract to serve 200, yet the city could not produce that many people for MAXIMUS to serve. They are inefficient and ineffective."[42]

Living on the Brink

Smaller community-based nonprofits, which have historically provided employment and training services to low-income populations, represent a large and diverse group nationwide. Before the 1998 Department of Labor legislation under the Workforce Investment Act (WIA; Public Law 105-220), 163 federal programs funded employment and training, and tens of thousands of nonprofit and for-profit organizations have received contracts and grants under these titles. In New York City alone, more than 115 individual providers had one or more employment and training contracts under federal titles before the newly awarded TANF contracts and the commencement of the WIA programs.[43] The providers' capacity and ability to compete in a more competitive and performance-based environment varies enormously, but most of the organizations we spoke to believed they would "get by" in the short run. Few small organizations had the ability to bid on the TANF contracts, given the scale and organizational capacity requirements. Those that did often did so as a collaborative. In San Diego, for example, a collaborative of nonprofits in the South Bay community bid as the Metropolitan Area Advisory Committee to serve that community. They did not, however, win the contract in San Diego and are currently litigating. In New York, where the bidding process was not the typical open competitive process but a negotiated acquisition, the city "invited" organizations to bid, and many historic small nonprofit contractors were closed out. Many small experienced providers lost their contracts with the city in what has been described as a "shake out."

Because of the scale of these efforts, however, most of the prime contractors in Milwaukee and New York by necessity have solicited or responded to CBOs' requests to act as subcontractors or to link with these organizations to provide training and support for clients with special training or social service needs. Under current bidding processes to select providers to service TANF clients, many historic providers will continue to serve portions of the caseload, albeit to a limited extent. There will be additional opportunities for many of them to compete for clients under WIA programs, but success under that system depends on the selection of a provider not primarily by the jurisdiction, but by the customer. Further, in the short run, many of the national for-profit providers (and large local nonprofits), such as Lockheed Martin IMS and MAXIMUS, have selected CBOs as subs, in part to mitigate the political backlash against them in the communities where they have won contracts. Subcontracts with CBOs have a number of valuable practical and political payoffs as for-profits enter new markets. First, in the short run they can learn from CBOs, who have a better understanding of particular client needs and connection to the resources in the community to serve them. Further, their association with well-known and trusted community organizations provides some political cover, helping to coopt and deflect criticism from groups that might otherwise be their opponents.

In the short run, then, many CBOs and smaller nonprofits may survive, even as they scramble to change their programmatic focus, seek other sources of public and private support, and serve the short-term needs of large contractors. Over the longer term most observers predicted that many of the weaker providers would scale back or close down. Since the industry varies enormously in quality and fiscal soundness, the consequences for many small providers may be dire. How that will affect the quality and range of available services appears to be mixed.

Many small providers serve populations with special needs. One small contractor who lost her contract when the city of New York reorganized its delivery system described it this way: "Good CBOs in communities are linked to providers and understand the needs of their clients. You have them and you know them. Some CBOs are bad, some mediocre, but CBOs have unique advantages."[44] For example, the Chinatown Manpower Project in New York has historically served Chinese-speaking clients whose ability and willingness to benefit from training and employment services provided by a borough-wide contractor under the new service delivery arrangements is limited. Whether current contracting and referral arrangements can preserve the services that may be critical to special populations located in particular communities is questionable. The results many fear may be that populations like ex-offenders, ethnic populations, and drug-addicted clients may be poorly served. Further, there is concern that welfare applicants from these special groups, when they are diverted to job placement and employment training, may simply disappear, falling through the cracks in a system that has no capacity to meet their special language and cultural needs.

In Houston, the career center contractor as well as interest groups fear the consequences of this shake-up. "In my opinion, when we lose the little guy [for example, the small CBO], we lose the hard to serve clients because that is who they trust and who they go to. They are not coming to my career center because I am there. They have to feel some reason to be comfortable and safe to come. When we lose the contract, we lose a lot."[45] Other observers viewed the possible thinning of the provider ranks as healthy, reducing the weaker and less able providers and strengthening the field more generally.

The smaller nonprofit contractors in Houston "do a lot more than what the performance standards measure," yet their dedication to their mission does not allow them to cut services even if current contract arrangements do not reimburse them for their additional costs.[46] Mission drives the service policies of SER-Jobs for Progress in Houston, but two of the smallest CBOs with contracts are being placed on probation and are threatened with contract revocation due in part to the difficulty they have had in getting their operations off the ground and in part to their unwillingness to capitulate on their service commitments in response to the economic realities of their contracts.

There is evidence that New York's HRA is worried too. Current contract designs that provide incentives for immediate placement and provide limited resources for longer-term support have not fared as well as expected. A recent summary report on placement and retention rates collected by the GAO found job placement rates among contractors to vary widely, but that only 9 percent of the New York City contractors met established level of placement. Only 36 percent met established job retention rates.[47] Monthly data provided by HRA for October 2001 indicated that ESP contractors had average placement rates of 29 percent and retention rates of 9 percent at ninety days and only 3 percent at six months. (Individual contractor performance varies greatly with retention rates at each milestone ranging from 2 percent to 28 percent and from 0 to 14 percent respectively.)[48] Houston and San Diego contractors fared poorly as well.[49] In New York, many viewed the poor performance, especially in job retention, as a result of the paucity of intensive services for clients with special needs. The providers most often serving these populations historically have been the CBOs.

So much controversy has attended the poor performance and the weak support for CBOs in the contracting system that the city of New York recently awarded, through a negotiated acquisition process, thirty new contracts to serve special populations under WIA. All thirty contracts were awarded exclusively to nonprofits—mostly CBOs. This represents a big victory for advocates who have questioned the viability of the current contracts to serve a caseload with significant labor market barriers. It also reflects the city's increasing recognition that job retention among all the contractors is too low. These contracts represent an additional city investment in CBOs providing support services for the most difficult and vulnerable parts of the caseload with multiple barriers. They already total more than $128 million and will provide significant cash advances, more adequate funding, regularized reimbursements, and a recognition of the more intensive service needs that some clients have to enter and retain employment.

While CBOs face considerable risks, they vary enormously in capacity, resourcefulness, and promise. Bill Grinker of Seedco/N-PAC described those nonprofits living on the brink as "a mixed bag in terms of capacity and ability to survive. Many will remain subs in the short run." The problem over the long run, as the for-profits develop capacity in the community, will be their declining need for these CBOs and their incentive to save the overhead devoted to managing them. Further, even for those who currently have contracts, there is a question about whether performance-based contracts will drive them out because of inadequate capital to sustain themselves while they await payment. Finally, Grinker questioned whether the for-profits would continue to need the political protection that they now enjoy through the connection they have with CBOs that serve as their subs. One long-term city employment contractor, which lost its contract when the city administration reorganized service delivery in New York, viewed the selection process as entirely politically motivated, granting new large contracts to mayoral favorites and politically connected for-profits and large established nonprofits. "What we will lose is the human element. Smaller providers are better than larger ones. Small nonprofits are driven by values and mission, and their staff is more concerned with people than numbers. All this gets lost in bigness—clients get lost."[50]

The HRA executive deputy responsible for designing the original contracts explained that the decision to select a few large contractors was based on a recognition that a major employment engine was needed to manage the large flow of clients and that would require providers whose scale of operations, systems capacity, and experience could manage in a performance-based environment. Nevertheless, the design made an explicit effort to protect the survival of the CBOs.

> Many nonprofits, especially CBOs, have limited cash flows, low surpluses, and no professionalized financial systems and management capacities to deal with performance-based contracts. A major idea behind these contract designs was to allow smaller nonprofits to work as subcontractors under the primes, and to reduce their exposure, to protect them and nurture them. They [the smaller nonprofits and CBOs] represent much of our infrastructure and infrastructure takes so long to develop . . . you don't want to lose community grounded organizations.[51]

Ironically, the CBOs view their exclusion as prime contractors in the selection process and their limited role as subcontractors as a repudiation of their contributions and the cause of their current problems.

One New York subcontractor described the situation facing nonprofit subcontractors as morally and financially untenable.

> The private and nonprofit contractors tend not to subcontract; the nonprofit contractors do more of it. In either case, prime contractor and subcontractor survival is predicated on doing as little work as possible. The city pays the primes only when they have certified that a recipient is in the labor force. For the average community-based subcontractor, $1,700 is received at initial placement, $1,300 at 90-day job retention and $200 at 180-day retention! Simple calculus coupled with the suspension of social mission drive the implementation of these contracts in one direction: *placement only*. . . . The subcontractors in these contracts are losing their shirts, both in financial terms and in the mutilation of their social missions, not to mention the morale of their staffs. . . . Hon-

orable community based subcontractors cannot in conscience, work in this way; and so through philanthropic help and often at serious financial peril, they cobble together literacy assistance, social services, child care, etc.[52]

Thus, while small nonprofits are motivated to stay alive and fulfill their missions, few have the resources and capacity to compete on their own, and many fear that even as subcontractors their future is in doubt. They complain of inadequate payment by the primes and of documentation and information processing demands that are as excessive and costly as when they reported directly to the city. In San Diego, CBOs receive referrals from the contractors with case-management contracts, but payments are capped and performance-based contracts may impose severe constraints on small organizations that must wait for payments until after a client is employed and retained for up to six months. In Houston, where the contracts for case management at one-stop centers merge TANF clients with others served under Department of Labor titles, clients themselves select the service providers that the city has qualified as eligible. Nonprofits and for-profit providers, therefore, compete for clients, and those with better connections and marketing expertise are likely to be the winners. Many CBOs have trouble competing in this environment.

Conclusion

Nonprofits are clearly sailing in uncharted waters. The new demands on nonprofits to compete in a reengineered welfare delivery system, where market forces compete with traditional values, has created real hazards. When missions collide with financial, managerial, and programmatic imperatives induced by new contractual arrangements, many nonprofits are forced to question their traditional roles as protectors of the poor and champions of progressive social values. Even so, many have adapted creatively to the new challenges, improving their performance, competing effectively on price, and developing innovative means to protect their missions. Many others, however, are struggling.

Much is made of the inherent disadvantages that many nonprofits have in the new welfare-service delivery markets where they now compete with large, national for-profit firms.[53] They lack management systems and information technology needed to manage large and complex contracts. They have comparative disadvantages in attracting top executives from government with welfare expertise, and they are constrained by their nonprofit status from raising capital in the financial markets. They lack the capacity and experience with the scale of operation that new contracts require. These are, indeed, formidable handicaps.

However, nonprofits in this industry have considerable strengths that national for-profit providers lack. As one nonprofit executive put it, "They're really known entities in the community that they serve, they have a respected level of cultural competence, they offer other kinds of services, you know, they already have pre-existing connections to the target populations that we're talking about. I think, in fact, they will do very well."[54] They have the ability to raise funds from both individuals and major philanthropic organizations. These resources allow them to enrich their programs and provide additional services that contract dollars might not cover. In these respects they can often provide higher quality services than their for-profit competitors.

However, nonprofits providing welfare services differ from one another as much as they do from their private-sector competitors. Many historic providers have been closed out of the reengineered delivery systems. As a consequence the adaptations nonprofits have made and their success in meeting the challenges show considerable variation. Some of the large experienced nonprofits have significant footholds in the markets examined in this study, and they appear to be holding their own. The speed with which all contractors have had to gear up, transform their systems, hire staff, and achieve placements has strained the resources of all contractors, profit and nonprofit. Early implementation has been rocky in many cases. While few data are available on the relative performance of individual contractors and subcontractors, information from New York and San Diego suggests that no single factor can explain the wide variation in prime contractor performance in placements and retention. There is no obvious or consistent pattern by size of contract, size of organization, or sectoral status.[55] Since in theory, in New York, referrals are randomly allocated by borough, differences in client characteristics cannot explain the bulk of the differences. Start-up problems—many of which were the result of the city's performance—no doubt explain some of the variations. However, nonprofits competing as primes appear, in general, no better or worse than their private-sector competitors.

Competition confronted these vendors initially when they responded to an RFP, and very few made the initial cut. Existing providers, therefore, are likely to be the strongest survivors. For example, Opportunities Industrialization Center (OIC) and UMOS in Milwaukee and Federal Employment and Guidance Services (FEGS), Wildcat, and Goodwill in New York are big operators that have had a long history of public service provision. These were the most likely to succeed. Thus the selection of a few experienced organizations, most of which were well-respected (and politically connected) providers in the community, left many CBOs and small and medium-sized providers out of the game. Their capacity and ability to succeed in a more competitive, performance-based environment vary enormously. Few even had the ability to bid on these contracts, given the scale and requirements for organizational capacity. Their roles as subcontractors have been more limited and their success is still in question. Little technical assistance or management support has been available, except in the few cases, like Seedco's N-PAC, whose very design is structured to allow it to play the role of a management services entity. Innovations like these, formed through collaborative and creative partnerships and assisted by private fundraising and changes in status (the development of a for-profit subsidiary), represent healthy and promising adaptations. However, these are the exceptions. Most smaller nonprofits are struggling. Squeezing profit margins will retard creativity and productivity among even the most competent providers. Worse, it will threaten the organizational missions and human services values that make nonprofit providers uniquely qualified to undertake some of the most difficult and important services provision now being outsourced. Those are the risks that attend the survivors. Others may simply disappear.

CHAPTER FIVE

For-Profits:
The Increasing Dominance
of National Firms

Human services are big business. The increasing corporate interest in human service markets reflects the size and potential profitability of the industry. In some service areas like home health and day care, private industry now dominates both nonprofits and government. As recently as 1992, private for-profit firms constituted 77.4 percent and 68 percent of providers in these two areas respectively.[1] Corporate interest in the welfare-to-work business is also growing, and as state and local governments have increasingly turned to outsourcing these services in response to the mandates of PRWORA, private for-profit firms have continued to capture an increasing share of the business.

Nonprofits still dominate in employment and training, but the corporate sector is giving them a run for their money. Peter Frumkin and Alice Andre-Clark report from their analysis of the U.S. Census Bureau's service annual surveys of 1992 and 1996 that the job training industry is experiencing an increasing growth in corporate providers. During the four year period after 1986–87 (predating the welfare reform legislation of 1996), revenues of for-profit firms grew at an annual rate of from 17.6 percent to 36.7 percent, while nonprofits grew no more than 13.2 percent. More recent data suggest that the expansion is continuing. From 1992 through 1996, the annual growth rate of revenues of for-profits ranged from 8.1 percent to 15.9 percent. This came at a time when nonprofit revenues grew by no more than 6.1 percent in any given year. Thus, between 1987 and 1996, revenues of for-profits tripled, growing to 39 percent of those of nonprofits.[2]

Most of the for-profits winning service contracts at the state and local level are national organizations whose experience and investment in the human services area had begun to grow significantly even before the passage of PRWORA (see box 5-1 and appendix B). Growth, particularly in the job training and readiness field, shows higher rates of increase among these for-profit providers than among the nonprofits, which had traditionally dominated this area of contracting.[3] MAXIMUS, Lockheed Martin IMS,[4] Curtis & Associates,[5] and America Works have clearly dominated the welfare employment field, with MAXIMUS and Lockheed pursuing mostly large welfare contracts in states and localities with big caseloads and America Works and Curtis & Associates concentrating on somewhat smaller markets. More recently, firms that have contracted to provide information technology, administrative services, and consulting have also begun to enter the service delivery portion of the field. Most notable have been the recent and high visibility contracts won by Lockheed Martin IMS. Lockheed Martin IMS has had a foothold in serving state and local governments in technology-driven service areas including human services and has recently entered the welfare employment area.

One for-profit provider described Lockheed Martin IMS's state of the art computer technology systems used, for example, in managing child-support collection systems around the country as "the Trojan horse they used to branch out into other areas such as the TANF contracts."[6] Dyn-Corp, headed by a former Lockheed vice president, is a recent entrant to the field. Anderson Consulting and Electronic Data Systems (EDS) are also becoming players in the broader human services areas, providing a range of services, but stopping short of providing direct employment training and placement services.[7] They engage in activities that run the full gamut: design, implementation, and management of information and technology systems. EDS, for example, has partnered with direct welfare service providers, such as with Goodwill in Milwaukee, to provide information and technology systems.[8] One public official in Milwaukee noted: "EDS and Lockheed made a deal with Employment Solutions [Goodwill's subsidiary], promising not to compete."[9] EDS subsequently became a subcontractor for two of the Milwaukee contractors, Employment Solutions and United Migrant Opportunities Services (UMOS).

Box 5-1. *Overview of National For-Profit TANF Employment Service Providers, 1985–2002*

Lockheed Martin IMS

Founded in 1984, IMS is a subdivision of the Lockheed Martin Corporation. One of five IMS divisions, the Welfare Reform Division established in 1996.

Government services: Child support, on-line government services, photo and ticket enforcement, assistance for emergency medical services, electronic toll collection, truck registration and inspection, and child support payments.

Growth of contracts: 1996—first employment service contract in Dallas; fall 1997—11 contracts in three states; spring 1998—17 contracts in four states worth a possible $36 million;[a] 2001—37 contracts in eight states worth a possible $108 million;[b] 2002—51 contracts and 36 project center locations in eight states.

Location and value of TANF contracts: 26 TANF contracts worth a possible $108 million, an increase of three times the potential value in spring 1998;[c] 85 percent of current contract value is with local sites in Florida and Texas; average current-year contract value is $4 million.

Growth of revenues: IMS is the fastest growing subdivision of the Lockheed Martin Corporation. Lockheed Martin's state and local business grew 32 percent a year after the company acquired the IMS unit in 1984.[d] Sold in 2001 to Affiliated Computer Services (ACS) for $825 million.[e] ACS reports revenues of $1.4 billion in six months ended December 31, 2001, an increase of 43 percent.[f]

MAXIMUS

Established in 1975 by David Mastran. Welfare Reform is one of four divisions of the Government Operations Group.

Government services: Government Operations Group handles child support collection and managed-care enrollment; Consulting Group handles information technology, systems planning, human services, e-commerce, organizational automation, and fleet management.[g]

Growth of contracts: 1988–93 contract with Los Angeles, first for-profit welfare contract; 1996—3 contracts worth $7 million; 1997—5 contracts in 4 states including the W-2 contract in Milwaukee; 1998—12 contracts in 7 states; 2002—38 contracts in 15 states worth a possible $85 million.[h]

Location and value of TANF contracts: 15 TANF contracts worth a possible $56 million, eight times the value of contracts held in 1996;[i] contracts in 10 states, four of them in California, and the largest ($14 million) in Milwaukee; average current-year contract value $3.7 million.

Growth of revenues: Started in 1975 with $12,000 and grew to $3.5 million in revenues by 1980.[j]

Revenues grew an average 36.75 percent a year, rising from $88.4 million in 1995 to $319.5 million in 1999[k] and to $487.3 million in 2001.[l] Some 56 percent of revenue produced by the Government Operations Group in 2001.[m]

Curtis & Associates

Founded in 1985. Acquired in March 2002 as part of the Concera Corporation.

Government services: Solely employment services with employment communication consulting and train-the-trainer options focusing on job retention, life skills, and professional staff development.

Growth of contracts: 1985—first contract, Nebraska Department of Health and Human Services; 1996—11 states, $9.2 million worth of business; 1998—15 contracts, over $29 million; 2001—37 contracts in eight states worth at least $60 million.

Location and value of TANF contracts: 31 contracts in 13 states worth possibly $65 million;[n] two caseload contracts with New York and one with Washington, D.C., compose 50 percent of the total value; average current-year value is $2,107,766 (without D.C. and New York, $1,181,402).

Growth of revenues: Information not available at time of publication.

ARBOR Incorporated

Founded in 1963.

Government services: Marketing and research consulting firm, education and training program, consulting and training organization based on customer satisfaction.

Growth of contracts: 2002—70 contracts, an estimated $16 million.

Location and value of TANF contracts: 1998—estimated 70 percent JTPA/WIA contracts; 2002—estimated 50 percent JTPA/WIA and 50 percent Welfare to Work.[o]

Growth of revenues: Company unwilling to provide revenue information.

America Works

Government services: Employment services contracts only.

Growth of contracts: 1984—becomes a for-profit organization and has a contract with New York City. Company unwilling to provide contract information.

continued on next page

Box 5-1. *Overview of National For-Profit TANF Employment Service Providers, 1985–2002 (continued)*

America Works (continued)

Location and value of TANF contracts: Serves welfare recipients through six offices in New York City (Manhattan and the Bronx), Washington, D.C., Yonkers, Albany, and Maryland.[p]

Growth of revenues: Grew 30 percent each year from 1984 to 1997[q] and had $7 million annual revenue.[r]

Notes

a. Rosabeth Moss Kanter and Courtney Purrington, "Lockheed Martin IMS: Making a Contribution and a Profit," Harvard Business School Publishing, December, 1999.

b. Contract information provided by Dr. Amy Zeitler, Lockheed Martin IMS, Business Development Manager.

c. Current contract information provided by Tom Scott, Lockheed Martin Contracts/Compliance Manager.

d. Information provided by Terry Lynam, Director of Communications, Lockheed Martin, as quoted in "Lockheed Martin Co.," *Washington Technology*, November 8, 1999.

e. "ACS Completes Acquisition of Lockheed Martin IMS," PR Newswire Press Release, August 24, 2001.

f. "ACS Announces Record Revenues, Net Income and EPS," PR Newswire Press Release, January 22, 2002.

g. Nina Bernstein, "Squabble Puts Welfare Deals under Spotlight in New York," *New York Times*, February 22, 2000, p. B1.

h. Contract information provided by Judye Yellon, MAXIMUS vice president, Workforce Services.

i. Contract information from 1997 to the present provided by Akbar Piloti, MAXIMUS executive vice president, Welfare Reform Division.

j. Frederic J. Rommer, "MAXIMUS Pulling in the Outsourcing Jobs," special to the *Washington Post*, September 20, 1999, p. F13.

k. United States Securities and Exchange Commission, Form 10-K, for fiscal year ended 1999.

l. United States Securities and Exchange Commission, Form 10-K, for fiscal year ended 2001.

m. Ibid.

n. Current contract information found on www.selfsufficiency.com/index.html.

o. Information provided by Peter Stroub, ARBOR Incorporated.

p. Prepared testimony by Peter Cove, founder, America Works, Subcommittee on Empowerment, U.S. House of Representatives, Hearings from the 106th Congress, Small Business Committee, May 25, 1999.

q. Information received from the interview with Peter Cove on CNN, "Who's in Charge," August 21, 1997.

r. Shannon Murray, "Bringing Opportunity to Welfare Recipients," *Baltimore Sun*, May 14, 1998.

Corporate players are changing the rules of the game in areas with a long and stable history of public-nonprofit partnerships. While many view their emergence in employment and training as a healthy development, likely to improve performance and reduce public costs, their participation is relatively recent and their impact uncertain. With little systematic evaluation of their strategies and service records, advocates of the poor, traditional providers, and policy observers question the wisdom of the speed and scale of current public contracting with private firms.

Four areas of concern dominate current discussions of the effects of for-profit firms when they compete with government and traditional nonprofit providers. For-profit firms move to service areas where their assets and expertise can maximize profits. In a changing social service environment where their presence is reducing public and nonprofit investments, will they stay the course, or will they exit markets when clients who are harder to serve reduce their profitability? Given their emphasis on reducing costs and increasing profits, can they be trusted to ensure the well-being of vulnerable clients? With increased comparisons between their performance and that of traditional providers that may have lower levels of capitalization and greater commitment to social-service missions, will the increasing dominance of for-profit firms crowd out nonprofits—especially CBOs—and, with their market power, draw needed talent away from them and government? Finally, will existing government oversight and monitoring functions be sufficient to ensure that necessary trade-offs between profitability and contract expectations protect the integrity of the contracts and the well-being of clients?

Business vs. Public-Service Goals

Most of the corporate literature, as well as interviews with national senior corporate executives and local site managers, reflect corporate philosophies, which wed public service goals with business goals. Companies varied in their strategies, degree of specialization, and target markets. Curtis & Associates, a small for-profit, has contracts in Waukesha, Wisconsin, and recently won two contracts in New York City that are exceptionally large for an organization its size—$26 million for assessment and job placement and $35 million for employment services and placement over three years (services reserved for clients who could not find jobs immediately following a four-week job-readiness program). These two three-year contracts, which represent more than fifteen times Curtis's average annual contract size, have necessitated subcontracts with six local vendors—all for-profit organizations.

While Curtis & Associates is clearly profit driven and evaluated the opportunity of these contracts on a financial basis, its approach is driven by the mission established by the company's founder, Dean Curtis, a former university professor and a motivational leader and company spokesman. Curtis's managers have internalized his values in the organization. "Dean has a mission. People do want to work. There is hope for the future gained through work. Hope and self-sufficiency are key."[10] Having been consultants who sold their program designs to other clients and contractors, Curtis executives have been well indoctrinated in the corporate mission and in specific programmatic philosophies. "Curtis & Associates will have an international impact on reducing poverty and unemployment. Through our efforts, people will have higher self-esteem, higher hope for the future, and jobs that will enhance their self-sufficiency. Governments and businesses will save millions of dollars through the efforts of our company."[11]

Similar in size and corporate philosophy is ARBOR, a private, Philadelphia-based firm with offices and contracts serving disadvantaged clients (not all TANF) in thirty locations around the country. One of its contracts is a large new three-year contract with New York City for $17.8 million to do initial assessments and job placements. Founded by psychologists almost forty years ago, ARBOR provides training and consulting and conducts behavioral research around the country. It describes its corporate mission as "maximizing the development of human potential in the workplace." Curtis and ARBOR have a motivational philosophy that is systematically integrated, substantively and symbolically, in numerous ways throughout their programs and internal management. These are not charitable organizations. Nonetheless, their literature and corporate presentation appears to be driven by a value-laden philosophy that is well understood and illustrated in practice. It is perhaps the corporate history of each that makes their motivation to be players in this growing industry most compelling. Both cited their comparative advantages as contractors, based on their experience and the superiority of their programmatic philosophies, rather than their technological or managerial superiority. This contrasted most sharply with the dominant players, MAXIMUS and Lockheed Martin IMS.

Dominating the Market: MAXIMUS and Lockheed Martin IMS

MAXIMUS and Lockheed Martin IMS are clearly the behemoths of the for-profit firms in the welfare reform area, and they seek the largest market shares and rates of growth. MAXIMUS, in particular, has the size and capital to move and gear up quickly in the welfare area, and these characteristics made it an attractive choice to San Diego, Milwaukee, and New York. Furthermore, it has the investment capital to survive a long time in a performance-based system, and its corporate representatives are well aware that the smaller for-profits and nonprofits simply do not have the same degree of leverage it takes to manage large caseloads under performance-based contracts. Awareness of their unique position among competitors has made them aggressive in undertaking rapid expansion. Remarks by George Leutermann, a human services professional with years of experience in both the public and nonprofit sectors,[12] and, until recently, the vice president of MAXIMUS's welfare reform division, contrast with those of executives of other private firms. "MAXIMUS will lose money for the first twenty-two months (of the New York City contract) and will make returns of 15 percent over the next thirty-two months. Firms like Curtis and Goodwill do not have the capital for those kinds of start-up investments." The MAXIMUS motto, clearly displayed on the company's corporate business cards and literature, is "Helping Government Serve the People." While corporate philosophy stresses that its "business is successful families and unconditional positive support—it's all motivational, it's self esteem, it's about relationships—that's what makes the MAXIMUS system work"[13]—it was the management and technological innovations that were described as distinguishing MAXIMUS from its nonprofit and public competitors and "sticks rather than carrots" that were identified as critical factors in its competitive advantages. "Good relationships with employers, an ability to sanction clients, discretion to hire and fire staff, business-like attitudes and a belief in what you do accounts for MAXIMUS's success. Government will not be flexible, MAXIMUS will be."

MAXIMUS stressed its growth strategy and its expectations to quadruple in size. Revenues grew an average of 36.8 percent a year, from $88.4 million in 1995 to $319.5 million in 1999. By 2001 it had revenues of $487.3 million. While not all of these revenues derived from welfare contracts, 56 percent came from the government operations group. (The government operations group alone had revenues that grew from $97 million in 1997 to $272 million in 2001, an average annual growth rate of 23 percent.) MAXIMUS had won fifteen TANF contracts estimated at about $56 million, or eight times the value of welfare contracts held in 1996 (see box 5-1). However, recent increases in the welfare reform division resulted from an increase in existing caseloads more than from new outsourcing contracts. President David Mastran explained this as a result of the current reluctance by states and localities to start new outsourcing programs.

The rate of expansion has been significant nonetheless, and the use of nonprofits and smaller proprietary providers as subs and partners is a short-term necessity to meet the service demands of many new contracts. In both Milwaukee and San Diego the use of subcontractors was very important—for increasing both capacity and breadth of services. However, local subcontractors—especially CBOs—were especially important for their political influence and their knowledge of the local culture and community resources.

> We made some stupid decisions by not understanding the culture—though we should have understood it. We were under great scrutiny politically, and the [state legislative] audits revealed some insensitivities on our part; MAXIMUS drops in a new place where politics and community relations can be a problem. There is a huge advantage to knowledge of the community and political culture. We've figured out how to tap that, either by collaborating with nonprofit subcontractors, or becoming a major subcontractor for a nonprofit prime."[14]

Even so, subcontractors, too, were held to performance standards: "There are explicit criteria that these subcontracts must reach through retention and number served. We are a business. We have a contract. We hold your hands to the fire. If you do well, you get a good reputation."[15]

"We are producing pretty well on all dimensions," reported Jerry Stepaniak, the current MAXIMUS vice president for the Welfare Reform division and also the local site manager in Milwaukee. "We have to do a good job; we are the poster boy for everyone [private contractors]. We are the easiest, most convenient target for critics. While the reverence of the mission is important to nonprofits, the mission here at MAXIMUS of doing a good job is not any different."[16] He pointed to the enormous advantages MAXIMUS has, especially in the early stages, with access to capital that allows it to make business decisions with short-term downsides, but big wins in the long term. It has the ability to hire enough seasoned professionals from both government and the nonprofit sector to bring in major-size projects.

In Arizona, for example, MAXIMUS was able to conclude a contract on January 6 and become operational on April 1. This included hiring one hundred workers, purchasing and configuring computer systems, undertaking staff training, and opening eight offices. "No other government enterprise could do it. There would be too many approvals needed and procedures to move that quickly."[17]

David Heaney, the MAXIMUS project director in San Diego (and a former Episcopal priest and executive director of Episcopal Community Services), painted a similar picture of MAXIMUS's comparative advantages, especially at start-up. The typical approach for MAXIMUS is to bring in an experienced transition team to set up a new site and then have them move on when the offices are operational. "The MAXIMUS team came in from all over the country to do everything. There was a count down and a set of generic policies and procedures that are operational around the country in every site. The site plan was 'boiler-plated,' leases negotiated, and we set up a regular 'war room' in downtown San Diego." Staffing was the biggest challenge.

> We were competing against all the other contractors. Lockheed tried to recruit a GAIN manager from the central region but after they reneged on their salary commitment they came to us. There is a leadership group in welfare to work, and all contractors are competing for them. We hired three county managers and the balance of our staff came from the nonprofits—very few from the private sector. MAXIMUS leadership makes it more attractive to come to us. The bottom line is not the only thing; we have the heart of a social worker but the head of a good business person.[18]

Other firms have similar advantages, albeit at a more modest scale of operations. America Works was an innovator in the supported work movement, where many of the work-first strategies were developed decades ago, as an early operator of a site in Boston when still a nonprofit. The CEO of America Works outlined the reasons it decided early in its existence to move from nonprofit to for-profit status:

There were lots of states interested in the kind of work we did, and
our board was young and entrepreneurial. But to build a nationwide effort, we needed to capitalize, to borrow and invest. We
wanted to raise money to grow and spread nationwide. The main
drive to become private was to raise money. That allowed us to
seek arrangements that shifted our contracts from line item to performance-based. That was unusual at the time.[19]

Introducing contracting arrangements that were performance-based was
indeed an unusual move at the time, but one that served as a good business strategy and distinguished America Works from its competitors.
America Works now claims to be growing at 30 percent a year.[20]

The supported work model, pioneered by Wildcat Service Corporation and the Vera Institute, was run as a demonstration in the 1970s by
Manpower Demonstration Research Corporation (MDRC). America
Works, when still a nonprofit, was an early operator for MDRC in
Boston. It remains philosophically attached to the model, which stresses
a method of training and support services for the disadvantaged that
embraces a philosophy that "work normalizes and socializes and creates
self esteem, but the real work starts when people start the job."[21] Thus
America Works had a unique message and means of working two
decades ago that has become the dominant paradigm of welfare reform
efforts nationwide.[22] Many providers now contract with multiple
employers and diverse industries and companies for providing on-the-job
support and counseling for job-ready clients that they place. Indeed,
while America Works is proud of its history, it readily concedes that there
is little variation in programming across providers: "Everyone knows the
same things." While America Works is confident of its role and ability to
deliver on its contracts, it is small compared with MAXIMUS and Lockheed Martin IMS, serving only 10,000 clients nationwide and placing
about 5,000 a year of both TANF and other DOL–financed clients. In
contrast, in the 2001 fiscal year, MAXIMUS reports 17,500 job placements of welfare recipients and 100,000 individuals in employment.[23]

More than most other for-profits, America Works has maximized the
opportunities that being a for-profit in this environment provides by
using tax credits (and some grant diversions), hiring clients itself, and
then placing them as temporary workers with contracted employers for
whom they can provide on-site supervision and support. Employers
have the opportunity to "try before you buy" in a three- to four-month

temporary arrangement. America Works pays the client with the fees paid by employers, but the wage rate they pay is less than the employer pays America Works for a temporary worker. Employers' costs can also be reduced through grant diversion. Thus America Works stands to profit from the placement beyond what the contract pays.

Some see this income maximizing behavior as detrimental to the client. Nancy Biberman, the executive director of WHEDCO, shared her views from a firsthand experience.[24] WHEDCO, a highly respected non-profit, was sought by America Works to partner with it in applying for a $30 million New York City contract. WHEDCO described itself as the poster child of employment and training providers, embracing a holistic approach to meeting clients' needs. An association with it would thus increase the visibility and legitimacy of America Works. In an arrangement brokered by the Local Initiatives Support Corporation, (LISC), a community development intermediary, WHEDCO developed a for-profit subsidiary to partner with America Works for its New York City contract. However, the relationship soured quickly. WHEDCO, the only partner of America Works, found that its service to clients was inadequate and its profit-maximizing behavior robbed clients of needed support services. Indeed, as a mission-driven nonprofit that served more than 50 percent of America Works' clients, WHEDCO had to cross-subsidize its payments per placement from America Works with other resources in order to provide the needed support services for its clients. "We barely broke even on the arrangement because we provided layer upon layer of solid supportive services. But it was our investment that made America Works's performance so good."[25]

WHEDCO terminated its relationship with America Works in 2001 due to serious differences in approach and philosophy. America Works objected to the time and cost WHEDCO incurred by providing additional social services, thereby hurting the "bottom line." However, WHEDCO claims that America Works's highly favorable performance outcomes reflect the significant investment WHEDCO made in supplementing services, and not in the placements America Works made itself. The strategy seemed to work. America Works outperformed all other New York City contractors on both placement and retention in HRA monthly performance data reported for October 2001.[26]

The dissolution of this relationship reflects considerable differences in values and approach, which many feel reflect profound cultural differences in the way different providers approach their work. WHEDCO was bound by its social-service mission and unwilling to capitulate to a bottom line regardless of the economic rationale for doing so. The tension between contractual requirements and mission appears less salient to private-sector contractors. Indeed, when Ed Gund, senior vice president and chief operating officer at IMS, was asked about the conflict between mission and contractual demands, he responded, "The quality and character of services are all contract driven. If you want a particular service, put it in the contract."[27] This was echoed by David Mastran, CEO at MAXIMUS: "What gets measured and rewarded gets done."

Use of mechanisms like grant diversion and forming a temporary employment agency, which were central to the America Works strategy, appear less popular among other firms. With the exception of Seedco's LLC and Wildcat Service Corporation, few have used these mechanisms as effectively, and some, like ARBOR, have rejected them outright, eschewing the documentation and loss in lifetime benefits that TANF clients experience when they use up precious months of their lifetime limit through grant diversion.[28] The clash of cultures, however, when for-profits collaborate with nonprofits is a more common theme. YW-WORKS in Milwaukee also formed an LLC with private-sector partners, but severed the relationship after the first contract period as a result of similar kinds of differences in style and values. David Heaney of MAXIMUS in San Diego stressed the importance of selecting subs with "services you need, political influence, a good fit philosophically and organizationally, and [a compatibility with your] culture."[29] However, private and nonprofit cultures seldom harmonize well.

The large for-profits dominating this field see their role differently from most of the nonprofits. "The county is our customer. There is a power inequality with the client, and we recognize it. But the client is not your customer. They are not paying you. We provide services for *our* client, which is the county. Our motto is: When you are doing something that is not in your contract, you are volunteering. The nonprofits have more flexibility."[30]

Management and Technology

It is no accident that several of the dominating firms leveraged their success in management information and technology systems to dominate the welfare reform business. Success in electronic benefits transfers and collections of child support payments positioned Lockheed Martin IMS and MAXIMUS, in particular, to capture the growing welfare market. With increasing numbers of clients to be served and the need for sophisticated computer and information technologies to find, track, and document client activities, these technology-driven firms had a profound advantage over smaller for-profits and even over many large experienced nonprofits. With government agencies unable to attract the technical personnel, in a highly competitive market, needed to upgrade their computer and management information systems quickly enough, or to retain adequate staff to service them, many local governments see the advantages of contracting for the systems high-tech companies can provide.[31]

Returning from a conference of government technology experts sponsored by *Governing* magazine, a MAXIMUS group president reflected, "A survey of CIOs shows that there is an overwhelming trend toward greater privatization of technological functions, that that form of business is favored and increasing in scope. Government is facing a complete collapse in information technology. Outsourcing is inevitable because of [the difficulty in] recruitment and retention of top people. Private industries like MAXIMUS can offer salary that is flexible, a creative environment, and stock options."[32] Lockheed Martin IMS and MAXIMUS have been particularly attractive for the full range of services they can provide, and some jurisdictions have contracted for eligibility and benefits determination services as well, in order to take advantage of these technological services.[33]

MAXIMUS has the contract for eligibility determination in Milwaukee and Maricopa County, Arizona, where it works side by side with government employees. In Arizona, MAXIMUS serves more than 3,000 families in a pilot program as part of Arizona Works, designed to evaluate the effectiveness of the private sector in achieving programmatic performance and administrative cost savings. It provides benefits, assessment, orientation, life skills, job readiness, and other support services, in addition to job placement and retention services. Recently it earned an incentive bonus of $1 million for exceeding minimum placement levels.[34]

Similarly, Lockheed Martin IMS has a pilot program to determine eligibility in Florida and is responsible for benefit determination as part of its contracts throughout most of Texas and Florida. These are services that require sophisticated technology and for which many other current for-profit players are unlikely to be competitive. To increase their comparative advantage in these areas, MAXIMUS and IMS (before its recent sale to ACS) have been systematically acquiring firms with supplementary and complementary expertise (see table 5-1 for recent acquisitions). Indeed, MAXIMUS acquired thirteen new companies over the past few years to bolster its competitiveness in consulting and technology-related government services. ACS also acquired six new companies in areas that complemented its business. When local jurisdictions contract with firms like MAXIMUS and IMS, they are often looking for solutions to problems that they have been unsuccessful in solving themselves. Significant error rates in benefit and eligibility determination, for example, often result in costly overpayments and sanctions from the federal Department of Health and Human Services. States often lack the systems and personnel to easily correct the problems. Thomas Grissen, president of MAXIMUS's Government Operations Groups, described a change in how government approaches contracting.

> In the past government would find a problem, formulate a solution to that problem, and then bid the needed solution out to companies. There has been a shift in this practice as there has been a collapse in the work force and its abilities to properly analyze and develop solutions to the problems government faces. As a result, government bids out the problem and asks for creative solutions to solve it. The winning company is then contracted with to implement the solution it developed. This relieves government of the burden of problem-solving.[35]

David Mastran, CEO of MAXIMUS, identified two areas that attract public officials to contracting with it: new functions and old functions where performance has been poor. "Our strategy is to go after business where there is a disaster or an expansion of services." Welfare reform represents a prime example of the latter, and child support collections the former. IMS and MAXIMUS also claim a comparative advantage in their internal management systems, which can produce what government wants. Mastran emphasized the three things government officials want to talk about when they pursue a relationship: increased quality of service, increased productivity, and reduced cost. In San Diego, for example, MAXIMUS cites its ability to keep costs low by having workers carry larger caseloads than would be possible in less well managed companies. "We are a high pressure organization. Our workers carry a caseload of 110 clients, while 35 to 40 are typical in nonprofits."[36] In many of its contracts, however, existing government workers are hired,

Table 5-1. *Recent Acquisitions of Selected Vendors*

Company	Description	Acquisitions
Lockheed Martin IMS/ACS	Premier service provider of business process and technology outsourcing solutions	2002: ACS acquires AFSA Data Corporation 2001: ACS acquires Lockheed Martin IMS, outsourcing (BPO) services unit of National Processing Company, government unit of SCT 2000: Intellisource, Birch & Davis 1999: Consultec
MAXIMUS	Leading provider of program management, consulting, and information technology services for state and local government	1998: acquires Spectrum, DMG, Carrera, Phoenix 1999: acquires CSI-MAXIMUS, Norman Roberts and Associates, Unison Consulting Group Inc. 2000: TMR, CCI, VRM, Asset Works, PSI, SPI
Curtis & Associates/ Concera	Specializes in contracting with federal, state, and local government agencies to provide a wide range of business process outsourcing solutions	Curtis & Associates was renamed Concera in 2002. In 1998, Benova, Inc., headquartered in Portland, Oregon, was acquired by AFSA Data Corporation, itself a wholly owned affiliate of FleetBoston Financial Corporation. Benova, Inc., acquired Curtis & Associates, headquartered in Kearney, Nebraska, in 2000. In 2002 Benova, Inc., Curtis & Associates, and the government contracting division of AFSA Data Corporation, headquartered in Long Beach, California, became the Concera Corporation. Concera specializes in contracting with federal, state, and local government agencies to provide a wide range of business process outsourcing solutions.

and, as Mastran described, about 5 percent quit. "But then," pointing to his contract in Phoenix, "there was a doubling of productivity."

When queried about the management strategies responsible for cost savings and productivity increases, Mastran listed five basic factors: pay bonuses, training, technology, top management, and the work environment. First, MAXIMUS uses a system of pay bonuses in which 8 percent of salaries is placed in a pool, and employees can earn it by reaching the performance schedule. This represents a 2 percent bonus, awarded each quarter. Second, there is a significant investment in training, and the training is tailored to performance evaluations. Third, computer systems are state of the art, providing immediate access to e-mail, the Internet, and case management information. Fourth, top management is experienced and seasoned, usually with long public service careers as senior managers in human services. Finally, workers inhabit physical environments designed to reflect a clean professional corporate work setting. "If you take workers and place them in a good environment, they will work better." The design of the physical environment is so central to its strategy that the company has internal rules, and every detail is prescribed for any new office around the country, including the lights, plants, and motivational posters (they are always framed).[37]

Both MAXIMUS and Lockheed Martin IMS pointed to the character of their work environments—even the prescribed dress of their employees—as key to sending a message to the clients they serve about the seriousness of their enterprises. All private providers contrasted their environments with those typically found in public facilities.

Provision of incentives for workers through bonuses and other symbolic and workplace rewards distinguishes private firms from nonprofits, although a few nonprofits have used monetary bonuses to reward extraordinary performance. Training and performance evaluation appear to be highly developed processes that set the management practices of private firms apart. Human resource investments appear to have significant payoff, and performance evaluations are key to management. At MAXIMUS in San Diego, the process was typical. There is a required performance measurement for each position that is tied to bonuses, but employee performance is also tracked and posted to direct training efforts. Training is designed for every level in the organization, including supervisory training for managers. Further, MAXIMUS has a highly developed internal information network that offers fifteen to eighteen courses on everything needed to succeed in the company. "The company has a full-blown human resources division, and its workers see MAXIMUS as a full-time career endeavor."[38]

Good management information systems allow considerable oversight of individual workers. Surveys of customer satisfaction are routinely undertaken (as well as surveys of employee satisfaction) to assess management practices. Obviously, private firms are most interested in the time and cost associated with job placements and the rate of placement and retention associated with each worker, since performance-based contracts pay in relation to success on these variables. However, they are also acutely aware of the way they are perceived by both their employees and their clients. Public relations is important, and large corporate providers of government services are well aware that their image is as important as their performance in securing and retaining government business.

The For-Profits Are Here to Stay

The welfare-to-work market for the two largest players, MAXIMUS and Lockheed Martin IMS, has been on "a steady slope,"[39] but there is evidence that their efforts may be reaching a plateau. Few new markets remain where either could continue its recent rates of growth. MAXIMUS in particular has articulated a growth strategy that emphasizes a focus on large volume to achieve economies of scale.[40] This market strategy is reflected in its success in bidding on and winning contracts that average $3.7 million a contract year.[41] Looking toward future markets, Holly Payne of MAXIMUS observed, "As far as other cities, Philadelphia maybe, Chicago might grow, but really the cities that we have now are what we are concentrating on."[42]

Lockheed Martin IMS's growth in this market has also been significant, representing a tripling of the value of welfare contracts since 1998.[43] Nevertheless, closer examination shows that 85 percent of its current contract value of $108 million is accounted for by contracts in Texas and Florida,[44] two states that have pushed hard to privatize welfare activities. Lockheed's share of these efforts has resulted in average contract awards in excess of $4 million each.[45] Although outsourcing welfare system and employment services remains prevalent throughout the country at both the state and local levels, few states seem willing to cede exclusive control over the welfare system to a single for-profit like Lockheed. Only in Florida does Lockheed retain a majority of the welfare-to-work contracts.[46] Lockheed serves local boards there in eleven project areas in thirty-one counties across the state that represented 80 percent of Florida's welfare population in 1999. According to former senior vice president Holli Ploog, "Lockheed Martin's approach was to develop a service, offer to sell it everywhere, and to own the marketplace for that service offering exclusively." Such was their niche-oriented strategy in welfare to work: Lockheed "is very rigid in its approach and offers only what it does well. . . . It won't bid where it [such a demand] does not exist."[47] Therefore, it appears that either Lockheed will need to be more flexible in its strategy of where to bid or it will face the threat of running out of sites in which it can import its blueprint.

With most of the large markets currently under contract and the caseloads continuing to decline in most states, areas of greatest growth are likely to be smaller municipalities or current contracts coming up for rebid.[48] These types of contracts would seem to favor smaller and mid-sized organizations such as Curtis & Associates, America Works, and ARBOR, Inc., whose organizations focus primarily on employment services and do not require the large economies of scale of the larger for-profits. Curtis & Associates, for example, has a wide range of contracts, with as many worth more than $5 million as are under $100,000.[49] However, even it has doubled the number of its contracts and revenues since 1998.

ARBOR also has seen significant growth in the field of TANF client services over the past four years, although no company representative was willing to provide specific information. This growth, ARBOR reports, has come from its strategy of shifting away from the dwindling Department of Labor grants that have been the dominant source of contracts for the company. In fact, ARBOR has shifted from 80 percent funding from DOL grants in 1995 to 65 percent of current revenues from services to welfare-targeted populations under TANF.[50]

A relatively new entrant into the field of employment services is Dyn-Corp Management Resources, Inc. (DMR), which is a subsidiary of DynCorp, a $1.9 billion information technology and outsourcing firm.[51] Holli Ploog, former senior vice president at Lockheed Martin IMS and now president of DMR, said that her company "is much smaller in its approach (as compared with Lockheed Martin IMS),"[52] seeking to fill in the niches of the existing market. Once the company is there in a jurisdiction, it identifies lots of services it can provide. Such an approach seems well suited to a strong economy that has led to a great reduction in the number of clients on TANF and a caseload of clients who are harder to serve and will need a more tailored system of services.

Whatever the ultimate distribution of companies in the welfare-to-work market, it is premature to predict the exit of the larger organizations. Indeed, they moved into the welfare market opportunistically, leveraging their expertise in large, technologically sophisticated social services. Both MAXIMUS and Lockheed Martin IMS have already begun to assess the opportunities for growth in other social service areas. MAXIMUS seems the most optimistic about the growth of the market, in what it sees as a $23.9 billion industry to administer state-operated programs, including Medicaid, Children's Health Insurance, Food Stamps, TANF, Child Support Enforcement, Supplemental Security Income, and other general assistance and social services.[53] Of those contracts, David Mastran of MAXIMUS predicted that $12 billion to $15 billion is possible for privatization.[54] In order to move into these new service areas, MAXIMUS has been busy acquiring an assortment of twelve different firms. It has continued to acquire companies to help bolster its consulting and government operations groups by providing specialized skills in everything from integration of school records to technology to track child-support payments. With an annual growth rate of 23 percent from 1997 to 2001 and more than $487.2 million in revenues (56 percent of which derives from the government operations group), it is not difficult to discern the reason for David Mastran's optimism.[55] Mastran joked that MAXIMUS would like becoming the fourth column of government: executive, legislative, judicial, and MAXIMUS.[56] Given the recent slowdown in the growth of contracts for outsourcing as the current recession endures (even as the size of caseloads has resulted in larger revenues under existing contracts), growth estimates may need to be revised downward. Even so, 2001's 18.6 percent increase in revenues indicates continued strength in all areas of the company's work.

Lockheed Martin IMS is also experiencing significant growth: 32 percent a year since 1984, representing the fastest growing subdivision of the $25 billion Lockheed Martin IMS empire, before its sale to ACS in 2002.[57] This success has been led by a continuous growth of the state and local government market. Now that IMS has become a division of Affiliated Computer Services, a Dallas-based outsourcing company, it is better aligned with the mission and culture of its corporate parent and could very likely experience greater growth. The majority of growth over the years has been in the more technological areas of photo enforcement and ticket processing, yet the direct services, such as child support programs under Audrey Rowe, remain very strong.

IMS and MAXIMUS have different cultures and orientations. MAXIMUS is largely a human services company acquiring the necessary technological heft it needs to dominate the human services industry. David

Mastran described how IMS and MAXIMUS are different. "MAXIMUS is a social work company that has gained technical capacities. Lockheed is a technical model trying to look like a social work outfit. We look at social helping and acquire the technology that helps to that end. MAXIMUS is 100 percent human services."[58] IMS is much smaller than MAXIMUS in the service areas in which they both compete.

Examining the welfare service contracts may reveal the early traces of a pattern, one in which large for-profit companies enter service fields that local and state governments may have a declining capacity to manage. These companies look for service areas and jurisdictions where their technological and management tools, and other advantages of size, seem to be of greatest value in creating significant economies. Eventually, the growth rate in a particular service area will plateau, through a combination of factors: the saturation of major contract sites and the reluctance of the remaining cities to choose privatization, for either political or ideological reasons. These large for-profit companies seem less likely to pull up stakes than to allow their existing contracts to draw down. The remaining welfare caseloads in the large sites where MAXIMUS and IMS are dominant has been greatly diminished, and the remaining population has significant barriers to employment. MAXIMUS and Lockheed Martin IMS, dependent on the economies that accrue from large contracts, seem ill suited for the remaining caseload, which would be better served by the smaller for-profits and nonprofits that have greater flexibility and ability to offer more intensive and specialized direct services. Further, with an effort by local governments to squeeze the margins, even as the service needs become more challenging, large companies will either look elsewhere or change their strategies. Recent evidence from MAXIMUS in Milwaukee and San Diego suggests that they are expanding their relationships with specialized nonprofits better suited to service a number of the special-needs populations.[59] Even so, their large contracts in sites like San Diego and Milwaukee have continued without much loss of revenue.[60] With the current recession and the potential reversal in caseload trends, the near term remains promising.

Nevertheless, the entry of these large companies into welfare services is still remarkably recent, and the deteriorating economy, coupled with some of the political liabilities that for-profit firms face when competing with nonprofits, has changed the challenges. As a result, the companies may choose to alter their service delivery strategy. For example, Holly

Payne suggested that MAXIMUS might consider being a subcontractor in future welfare contracts as a way to avoid the costly public backlash and lawsuits involved with having a for-profit offering direct social services. David Heaney, MAXIMUS's project director in San Diego, estimated that welfare reform contracts generate only about 15 percent of MAXIMUS's revenues, but account for 98 percent of its legal costs. Lockheed Martin IMS already finds itself in such a position in Hillsborough County, Florida, where it serves as the subcontractor to Goodwill Suncoast, Inc. Though this arrangement was not Lockheed's original intent, the contract seems to serve it well. Assuming the role of a subcontractor capitalizes on the company's ability to provide technological services expertise, where it has continued to be dominant. If these approaches are explored, a new wave of contracts for these two for-profit behemoths could emerge, strengthening their dependence on and relationships with nonprofit partners.

Thus long-term strategies include diversification and a more centralized approach to evaluating business opportunities.

> We're here to stay, but we're going to be very careful about the sites we choose. We want to be thoughtful about where to invest. Historically, MAXIMUS has had a decentralized marketing strategy—the message was to be on the lookout for business opportunities. Now, however, proposals will be scrutinized carefully, rigorously, and centrally. Contracts are renegotiated from time to time, and we will not get involved if it is uneconomic. But our infrastructure allows us to do things that would be uneconomic for the nonprofits. It won't do anyone any good for the county to price us out—even when the caseload declines. We'll be around as long as they want us to be.[61]

Scale is important, however, and MAXIMUS is usually looking for a contract of at least $1 million. The optimal opportunity is one that allows a bundling of multiple services, which provides scale. "We would love to get a contract in which we can bring all the parts of MAXIMUS to the table. If we could get a site that would allow us to do childcare, welfare, and other services, we could really look to make a huge difference."[62]

However, there is evidence that private contractors are already moving beyond their TANF contracts to expand in the work-force development area under WIA funding streams (see table 5-2). Curtis & Associ-

Table 5-2. *Contracts by Type, Selected Vendors*

Provider	WIA	TANF	TANF and WIA contracts	One-stop contracts	Other
Lockheed/ACS	2	4	—	26	4
MAXIMUS	2	22	8	—	—
Curtis & Associates	2	26	4	2	7

ates, IMS, and MAXIMUS have multiple contracts around the country, many using both WIA and TANF funds. Curtis & Associates currently operates two one-stop centers, and IMS operates twenty-six, which are required of the states to receive WIA funds. In some cases, like Houston, the one-stop contracts serve both TANF and other eligible nonwelfare clients; in others there are separate points of entry. These represent large new expansion markets. Further, it seems clear that many states not now contracting for eligibility and benefits determination may be permitted to do so in the future. A Republican administration will be sympathetic to states' efforts to contract for these services, the eligibility determination portion of which is now allowed only through waivers. President Bush himself, while governor of Texas, applied for permission under federal waivers to contract for eligibility determination. While Texas's application was denied, it seems likely that HHS may be more favorably disposed to reducing these restrictions in the future. Furthermore, states not now allowed to contract for eligibility determination services for federal Food Stamps, SSI, and other programs may ultimately have the option to do so. These services, when bundled with welfare to work services, offer huge potential new markets for both MAXIMUS and IMS that capitalize on their technological strengths. Jerry Stepaniak, MAXIMUS vice president for welfare reform, reflected on the huge potential of loosening restrictions on contracting for eligibility determinations. Expanding into eligibility determination could by itself result in a two- to three-fold increase in the market sector from new contracts for these functions.[63]

Conclusion

Welfare reform has been good to the private sector. The systems restructuring that it has spawned in states and localities has allowed private companies to move aggressively to enter new markets in the employment services industry. Their rates of growth mirror changes in the policy environment predating the actual legislation of 1996. The landscape for contracting out has altered, and for-profit firms have established a formidable presence in markets historically dominated by nonprofits and public agencies.

A number of factors have helped the growth of for-profit firms. First, they were well positioned to enter a new contracting environment where performance-based contracts favor vendors that can make large initial investments. Well-capitalized companies were more nimble, capable of gearing up quickly to serve new markets with large caseloads under pressure to meet new federal placement requirements. Armed with technological heft needed to manage large contracts and with competitive power to attract experienced managers with knowledge of local markets, a number of large companies were awarded large, multiyear contracts to serve TANF clients. Their size, experience, and management systems made them an attractive choice for local decisionmakers seeking liberation from the costly administrative burdens of service provision and the onerous contract management functions typical of historic delivery systems.

In most large welfare markets, however, private companies do not have sole-source contracts. Local politics, risk aversion, and a commitment to introducing competition have conspired to induce public agencies to contract with multiple providers. In many cases this has meant awarding contracts to private and nonprofit organizations in the same market. In a few cases, like San Diego and Arizona, public agencies compete as well. When for-profit firms compete with other providers, their comparative advantages—and weaknesses—are often more clearly revealed.

Perhaps the greatest liability facing for-profit firms in human services is their political vulnerability. The public respects their know-how, but suspects their motivations. The behavior of for-profits, especially in human services, is heavily scrutinized. There is good reason for concern. Scandals in the health-care industry and in nursing home and child-care settings remain etched in the public's memory. These are not merely concerns about fiscal integrity, but about the ability of private firms to ensure the well-being of vulnerable populations when profit making drives their behavior.

Human services have a long tradition of public and nonprofit provision, and the service mission that characterizes them provides both trust in their motives and considerable protection from critics, even when their performance lags. Not so for the profit-making firms. Indeed, most project managers identified the risks and political pitfalls, often unanticipated, that accompanied their early operations in new markets as highly damaging. While public officials have recently favored private providers in their selection process, there remains considerable public distrust of the motives and practices of for-profit firms in the human services industry. So vulnerable were they to negative public relations, often emanating from their ignorance of local political and cultural norms, that several executives contemplated potential changes in their market strategies that would reduce their visibility. Indeed, some have suggested that they might favor sub rather than prime contracts.

Changes in policy are likely to be affected by the state of the economy that determines the size and characteristics of the caseload. Small caseloads are less attractive to large national for-profits that benefit from economies of scale. As caseloads decline and clients who are harder to serve—those with multiple barriers to employment—predominate, for-profit firms have fewer comparative advantages. Their early responses suggest they will increasingly partner with specialized nonprofits and CBOs whose expertise in serving special populations may be increasingly important to ensuring adequate placements under performance-based contracts. Ultimately, they may find remaining markets uneconomic and seek opportunities where they can use their technological advantages and exploit economies of scale. However, contracts for eligibility and benefits determination for state and federal income assistance programs may provide more attractive future markets for private vendors. In the meantime, all reported their intention to remain in this market.

Private vendors with the aggressive growth strategies of MAXIMUS and Lockheed Martin IMS prosper when they move quickly to capture new profitable opportunities. If David Mastran is correct, and future public service privatization opportunities may constitute as much as $12 billion to $15 billion of the $30 billion market in state and local services currently being provided, it seems unlikely that they will remain in a market where profitability declines.[64]

State and local governments are losing their capacity and the nonprofit infrastructure on which they have traditionally relied through the competitive forces that privatization has unleashed. The exit of these providers would have a serious destabilizing effect on the continued ability of local governments to provide services that are critical to vulnerable populations. There may be serious service gaps and dislocations that cannot be filled easily by nonprofits whose capacity has been greatly diminished or by public agencies that are increasingly out of the business. These threats are not immediate, but they are real.

Competition from the private sector appears here to stay, whatever its impact on nonprofit and public capacity. Contracting out is increasingly popular with state and local governments, and public officials are attracted to the cost savings they believe for-profit firms achieve and the flexibility they offer to scale up or down in response to local needs. Performance gains may be less clear.[65] Nonprofits and public agencies appear to be induced to improve their management systems and technological capacities under new contracting arrangements, especially in response to being compared with private providers. Generally, however, those nonprofits that have won contracts are already of a certain size and capacity to compete. Performance data were available, but there are significant limitations to using them to make conclusions about who performs better. As the data on America Works demonstrate, the performance of the for-profits may reflect the efforts of their partners as much as or more than their own efforts. Or worse, the performance data may merely reflect sophisticated subversion of contractual intent through creaming or manipulation of reporting. Even so, few consistent patterns reveal themselves. The answer to the question about how well for-profits perform when compared with their nonprofit competitors remains equivocal: it all depends.

CHAPTER SIX

When the Private Sector Competes: Challenges and Risks

In all the sites studied, the entrance of the for-profits is inducing profound changes in management practices and organizational adaptations of competitors. Not only are practices changing, but the nature of the discourse about public service is changing as well. While there are serious questions about whether or not the private sector will come to dominate this area of service delivery, there is no doubt that expectations of government performance and the roles of each sector in meeting social needs are shifting profoundly. These shifts appear to be here to stay, and, regardless of the ultimate balance of providers in the broad array of traditional public service functions, private-sector practices are forever altering the traditional values that have dominated public-sector provision.[1]

The private sector has been increasingly focused on the potential market that a huge public sector provides in countless service areas. The future role of the private sector is likely to be dictated by the size of the contracts and the efficiencies that private firms can realize in this market. With declining caseloads anticipated over the next few years (assuming a strong economy and increasing reductions of large numbers of easy to place clients), the size and character of this market may indeed be less attractive and responsive to the advantages that large, technologically sophisticated contractors can provide. Should the for-profits reduce their focus on this market (a not unrealistic expectation), remaining potential providers may be hard pressed to meet the continuing needs of a caseload with severe barriers to employment. If the public agencies have been drained of expertise and institutional memory and the bulk of smaller nonprofits have been weakened or have refocused on other service areas, the industry may very well be bereft of capacity and adequate competition to provide quality services in a cost-effective manner.

Even so, the market has been altered and the behavior of nonprofits, both large and small, is likely to be changed forever. In *Tides of Reform,* Paul Light analyzed the nature of reform pressures and their consequences for the future of the nonprofit sector.[2] Competing with the private sector induces its own kind of "reform." My reconnaissance uncovered patterns of change and likely consequences for the performance and future of both public and nonprofit organizations that bear continued scrutiny. My conclusion will suggest some of the effects of these changing relationships among players in the welfare-reform market and the risks they pose for the future. Longer-term analysis will be necessary to evaluate these risks, but this reconnaissance has provided strong indications of the direction of change and areas that should bear continued scrutiny.

Management and Organizational Adaptations

Paul Light's book on the tides of reform in the nonprofit sector points to pressures nationally from funders, volunteers, clients, boards, and professionals to improve performance, accountability, effectiveness, and discipline in their organizations. While multiple and complex forces have converged to induce nonprofits to reform themselves, the increasing competitive pressure from the private sector (and from governments evaluating the fitness of and relative returns from competing contractors) appears to be having an important effect on management practices.[3] While there are observers who have concluded that nonprofits can never win an efficiency battle with for-profit firms, those competing in the welfare-to-work arena are clearly aware that they must try.[4] Investments in management information systems, technology, professionalization, and sophisticated financial accounting systems appear to be a few of the ways that nonprofits "living by their wits" are adapting to the changing environment precipitated by competition and performance-based contracts. Sister Raymonda DuVall of Catholic Charities in San Diego described it best as a "paradigm shift." She described an effort to change a perception of her organization, held by people both within and outside the organization, as a bunch of "do gooders" with poor organization and fiscal structure, to that of an organization competing on a level playing field and driven by the tremendous pressure to succeed.

> We have a lot at stake, if the profits are going to invade, we've got to do it. Now our operational stuff is in sync with the for-profits, and we can work together. The lessons [of management reform] have changed us and how we behave in other spheres. We look at things differently than before in terms of accountability, managerial resources, quality assurance, and data collection and measurement. We have brought about a culture change. We built a corporate identity from our mission that readied us for changing our management.[5]

Management systems were already in place for most of the nonprofits that won contracts in the cities studied, and many represented large, old-line organizations—Goodwill and Federal Employment and Guidance Services in New York, the YWCA in Milwaukee, and Interfaith in Houston—with decades of contracting experience. For these, the threat is "mission drift" as they scramble to conform to programmatic requirements and contractual demands that may lead them away from their principal missions. Many others have far smaller asset bases and have undertaken contracts that are many multiples of their historic budgets (see appendix A). While continued pressures to perform side by side with the private sector induce changes in management systems and operations, the critical question for both private and nonprofit organizations is how to deliver quality services to an increasingly disadvantaged caseload at current payment levels and with increasing pressures to cut costs. While there are still indications that innovative programming and service arrangements are possible for organizations with multiple funding streams, the numbers of surviving organizations are likely to continue to decline, and few will be able to undertake the risks of new program models if they depend on resource streams from government contracts alone.[6] For the nonprofits that retain business only as subcontractors, there is a real question about how much longer the prime contractors will need them as caseloads decline and whether they can sustain themselves under the existing payment arrangements and reporting requirements as referrals decline and clients who are harder to employ predominate.

Creative efforts to provide technical assistance and fiscal and managerial support to smaller CBOs appear to depend principally on the availability of outside funding like that raised by Seedco's Non-Profit Assistance Corporation. Such efforts may have the potential to sustain quality operations that require focused initiatives, organizing smaller organizations in collaborative arrangements where they can collectively share resources and management systems. William Grinker has developed the logic of such arrangements.[7] Networks of agencies can consolidate functions, share administrative tasks, and collectively improve their position to attract funding, contracts, and capital financing. Some cost sharing, particularly of expensive and necessary overhead, can help financially strapped smaller agencies that might be better able as a collective to compete for the available resources of intermediaries. It is nonetheless a potentially fruitful strategy for strengthening the survival of experienced, mission-driven organizations threatened by new contracting arrangements. Grinker compares the winnowing-out scenario in managed care with that of the work-force development system, where, over time, players were sorted out and fewer providers left standing. He describes the system as one of "survival of the fittest." Unfortunately, however, the fittest does not necessarily equate with the fittest to deliver quality services, just the most nimble financial operators.[8]

"Brain Drain" and Public Capacity

In the case of for-profits and nonprofits that have survived the current challenges of competition, the need to staff up quickly to meet the expected client referrals has created a strain. In some sites, like San Diego and Houston, both the for-profits and the nonprofits are hiring county workers who will be bound by corporate performance standards and will thus sacrifice the security they once enjoyed in public organizations. Attracting and motivating key executive and managerial personnel has been difficult. In many markets, both private and nonprofit firms are competing for the same managers and job developers. As public agencies reduce their own efforts in this area, attracting former managers and executives from the public sector becomes increasingly competitive. Although a number of smaller for-profits claim that they do not outbid their nonprofit counterparts, this clearly does not characterize the strategies of the larger companies like MAXIMUS and Lockheed Martin IMS.[9] The larger companies have been successful in attracting former local welfare commissioners and senior public managers with experience and knowledge of the local markets they are entering. Ed Gund, the chief operating officer at Lockheed Martin IMS, described its senior staff as embracing a "public service mission." "Their backgrounds, largely from the public sector, attract them to Lockheed to achieve public service goals without many of the bureaucratic constraints to performance they experienced in government." He argued that they do not agree to work for Lockheed for the money. Nevertheless, salaries for senior executives at Lockheed Martin IMS are multiples of what most senior managers earned in the public sector. However, the competition for talent among the nonprofits has been fierce. Some companies, both the for-profits and some of the larger nonprofits, have reward systems that pay bonuses to job developers for job placements over a minimum. In one nonprofit some of the successful job developers had salaries plus bonuses that were in excess of six figures.[10]

Many of the for-profits viewed their organizational culture and the opportunity for public service–oriented managers to have more autonomy as highly attractive to former government employees and newly minted public policy graduates. Many executives viewed the opportunity to provide quality services with fewer bureaucratic barriers as well suited to a public service–oriented manager. Some of the smaller nonprofits, especially those that did not use monetary incentives to attract talent, felt their values, their missions, and the quality of their operations gave them a comparative advantage over private-sector organizations. While each pointed to the special features that distinguished his or her work environment, all were recruiting and hoping to attract similar kinds of employees, many of whom had or would have typically worked in the public sector.[11]

Though this study focused on a relatively limited number of cases and contractors, many top managers and site directors had been recruited directly from senior government positions or nonprofit leadership roles to lead a private contractor's operation. San Diego is illustrative. Sally Hazzard, the director of Lockheed Martin IMS's San Diego contract, was a former project director of CalWORKs, operating two of the county's six regions before she left to run Lockheed's operation in San Diego.[12] David Heaney, MAXIMUS's San Diego project director, was recruited by MAXIMUS when he was executive director of Episcopal Community Services. A retiring county official with executive responsibilities for CalWORKs at the San Diego County Health and

Human Services Agency, who had not quite decided what to do after leaving his county position, revealed that he was being aggressively courted by one of the larger private contractors and was likely to accept.

These patterns reflect Paul Light's findings among cohorts of policy school graduates and may simply represent a movement of talent to new loci of public service. With a free flow of talent across the sectors and increasing professionalization in all the sectors, there may be a desirable transfer of ideas and best practices over rather porous boundaries, improving the overall performance in all sectors. If, however, there is a hierarchy in the relative attractiveness of the various sectoral settings, and if, in the contracting environment, private organizations have a comparative advantage, there may be a further weakening of public institutions and nonprofit capacity.[13]

Some have argued that the current recessionary environment and a growing pool of graduates from professional schools increasingly focused on training nonprofit managers may be invigorating the prospects for reseeding the talent pools of both the public and the nonprofit sectors. Historically the public and nonprofit sectors have been particularly hospitable destinations for a diverse work force of new immigrants. With an increasing diversity in the workplace of the children of new immigrants, there may be some reasons for optimism.[14]

Even so, this reconnaissance has raised considerable concern. Whatever the relative advantages of the private contractors in attracting managerial talent, all are draining talent from the public sector. Whether this "brain drain" will weaken the capacity of government to be "smart buyers" and sophisticated contract managers or reduce its ability to reclaim many of these functions, should contracting arrangements prove unsatisfactory, is an important question. Clearly, government's attractiveness to talented managers has been declining for some time.[15] Major changes (many of which preceded the privatization of these functions) are exacerbating the problems of attracting able government employees. The acceleration of contracting out in the human services arena may ultimately limit government's options and reduce its capacity still further.

Contracting out can provide cost savings and improved performance, but only if government is a smart buyer and a sophisticated contract manager. Selecting the appropriate providers and designing contracts that provide the right levels of incentives to produce the desired outcomes is a challenging enterprise, as much art as science. It often takes experience over several contract cycles for public managers to refine the contract specifications in order to balance the needs of vendors with the proper incentives for performance and means of ensuring accountability. When public agencies lose their talent, they lose the experience and institutional memory necessary to manage the process and the opportunity to produce good performance in a cost-effective manner. Reduced capacity to manage the entire contracting process threatens the quality improvements and cost savings that contracting can provide.[16]

Accountability

Contracting for services, whether from private or from nonprofit providers, relinquishes public control over delivery and, under performance based contracts, the particular character and choices of services. Performance-based contracts introduce into public management market incentives that are thought to reduce costs, induce innovation, and generally improve outcomes by providing financial incentives to develop better models of service delivery capable of resulting in quicker, better, and longer-lasting job placements. But the incentives of performance-based contracts may also induce perverse behavior among providers, to reduce needed but more costly services, quicker rather than better and more lasting placements (beyond the bonus period), and preferences for clients who are easier to place rather than those with multiple barriers (and thus those in more need of costlier interventions). Indeed, there is a tension between "tightness" with respect to performance outcomes and "looseness" with respect to the means contractors are allowed to use to achieve them.[17] Financial incentives may induce contractors to rob clients of needed services that may affect their long-term well-being and, in some cases, their willingness or ability to participate at all. Clients with multiple barriers, such as language, drugs, and cultural differences, may not be receiving what they should. If they simply fall through the cracks or wind up worse off after the critical payment points are reached, contractors cannot be held accountable for their decisions.

Private contractors varied in the degree to which they defended their behavior on the basis of social mission rather than contractual obligations. Most nonprofits argued that their missions and values distinguished them from the private providers in just these ways.

Goodwill works for the clients, their welfare is paramount. We are here and will be here when the money dries up. We have to—the for-profits will only be here for the profit. Placement of clients is important, but in the long run [the goal is] to keep and grow in a job, and there is no money for long-term retention. Need sets vary among clients and thus we need to cross subsidize from other grants to cover costs.[18]

Even so, both private and nonprofit providers denied clients needed services for which they were eligible in Milwaukee.

Accountability for the quality and appropriateness of contractors' behavior (both programmatically and fiscally) creates measurement problems for public entities monitoring performance.[19] Public capacity problems, particularly with the size of the current caseload services, plague oversight quality, timeliness, and sanctions. While public agencies have reduced both direct services and the number of contractors they have managing welfare employment services, they have also reduced the size, experience, and quality of staff needed to design and properly manage these large and complex contracts. In all of the sites in this study, a GAO site visit confirmed the range of accountability lapses in monitoring, procurement, oversight, and performance that I uncovered in my reconnaissance.[20] In New York, where the strategy was clearly to reduce contract management by selecting fewer primes that are responsible for managing the accountability of their subs, the Human Resources Administration (HRA) has been focused almost exclusively on job placement and caseload contraction. Most of the emphasis is on automated systems for financial accountability. Even there, however, it is unclear whether increased investment in staff training and skills will be adequate to carry out their new functions. Further, recent indications are that even the accountability functions presumably met by the performance standards are to be compromised in the city's plans to renew contractors despite poor performance.[21] Thus a major rationale for performance-based contracting has been undercut in New York as it was in Milwaukee, where all contractors had the right of first acceptance in the contract renewal process because the performance standards were set so low and the numbers were so manipulable. Whether these outcomes reflect organizational ineptitude, political constraints, or a recognition that service disruptions would be too damaging if contractors were actually punished, these experiences raise serious questions about the improvement in accountability under current contracting reforms and the public capacity to ensure it.

The current contracting environment, with the large contracts selected through negotiated acquisition, has been described by a city official as a "sea change that has shaken up the employment world. It will result in less oversight and reduced monitoring."[22] These problems reflect a potential misunderstanding by government entities about the need that outsourcing creates for public agencies to increase their oversight role. "The idea that transfer of responsibility from the public to the private sector allows government to withdraw from oversight, reduce staff, and place sole or even primary responsibility for accomplishment of public policy objectives on private service providers is an invitation to trouble."[23]

Conclusion

This study has highlighted both risks and rewards from the dramatic changes taking place in the systems that deliver employment and training services to welfare recipients. Some of the potential consequences have significant implications for the entrance of the for-profit sector into other arenas that have historically been dominated by the public and nonprofit sectors. Several tentative conclusions seem warranted at this point. Public capacity is waning under increasing contracting. The future of mission-driven nonprofits is uncertain and worrisome. While systems of managed competition with the private sector are clearly improving the management, capacity, and performance of many fiscally sound nonprofits, many others are in danger of "losing their souls" and distorting their missions. Still others, living on the brink, are in danger of extinction.

Market forces alone are likely to drive the large national for-profits to arenas where their comparative advantages make them dominant. When caseloads decline and easier-to-place clients are scarce, the for-profits are likely to move on to other human service areas where they can increase their market share, economies, and profits. Given the reduced capacity of public agencies and the declining participation of CBOs, threats to a healthy service sector and to meeting the needs of a diverse client base are evident.

The declining attractiveness of employment in public organizations and the competition for talent in stronger nonprofits and private organizations gearing up for large new contracts threatens to leave government organizations bereft of talent. They also show symptoms of increasingly declining institutional memory and capacity for resuming service functions. Should the availability of competent and highly performing contractors decline or shift to alternative service areas, this "brain drain" will threaten the public ability to provide quality services to vulnerable clients.

Market incentives generated by the increasing popularity of performance-based contracts are inducing innovation and desirable management changes in many nonprofit providers. However, they are also producing distortions of contractual intent by motivating both nonprofit and private contractors to make choices about service delivery that may compromise the well-being of clients in order to minimize costs. Minimizing cost may inadvertently be threatening service quality and ultimate client outcomes. As the caseload gets smaller and the harder-to-serve predominate, the economics of quality service may simply prohibit existing payment schedules and contractual design.

The desire to reduce the public payroll and the functions and administrative burdens of public agencies may be creating serious potential accountability problems. Contracting requires more, not less, oversight. Contract monitoring has failed to keep pace with the size and complexity of system changes. Without adequate monitoring and program evaluation, the important virtues of contracting may well be lost and the ability of public agencies to protect their citizens and select among providers by both quality and cost may be sacrificed.

The increasing backlash of public employee unions, CBOs, and other local political powers against the private sector's incursion into their traditional domain has made entering new markets costly and uncertain for the larger for-profits. As a result, they may be forced to change their strategy or look for areas that are less highly politicized.

County Contracts

Contractor	Sector	Contract size	Assets	Income
Milwaukee				
Contract period 2002–03				
YW-Works	For-profit	$65,252,410	n.a.	n.a.
UMOS	Nonprofit	$66,517,591	$20,391,592	$10,031,453
OIC of Greater Milwaukee Inc.	Nonprofit	$36,940,478	$1,036,517	$33,363,611
MAXIMUS	For-profit	$36,940,478	n.a.	n.a.
San Diego				
Contract period 1998–2002				
ACS[a]	For-profit	$26,442,940	n.a.	n.a.
MAXIMUS	For-profit	$23,967,062	n.a.	n.a.
Catholic Charities	Nonprofit	$11,018,718	$8,347,702	$12,650,131
San Diego County Agencies	Government entity	n.a.	n.a.	n.a.
Houston				
Contract period 2000–01				
Houston Works	Nonprofit	$6,988,386	n.a.	$24,000,000
SER-Jobs for Progress	Nonprofit	$1,311,072	$1,176,734	$3,144,020
Lockheed/ACS	For-profit	$3,695,022	n.a.	n.a.
Interfaith	Nonprofit	$4,741,718	n.a.	n.a.
Gulfcoast Careers of Harris County	Government entity	$3,463,901	n.a.	n.a.
Community Services Program of the AFL-CIO	Nonprofit	$582,768	$379,645	$1,563,779

Contractor	Sector	Contract size	Assets	Income
New York				
Contract period 1999–2002				
SAP Contractors				
Association for Research & Behavior	For-profit	$17,797,500	n.a.	n.a.
Curtis & Associates[b]	For-profit	$26,932,500	n.a.	n.a.
FEGS	Nonprofit	$20,160,000	$80,419,722	$100,282,051
MAXIMUS	For-profit	$3,000,000	n.a.	n.a.
Goodwill Industries	Nonprofit	$35,437,500	$27,287,285	$39,386,149
ESP Contractors				
America Works of New York	For-profit	$30,630,000	n.a.	n.a.
Career and Educational Consultants	For-profit	$14,355,000	n.a.	n.a.
Consortium for Worker Education	Nonprofit	$8,250,000	$33,836,345	$7,531,841
New York Urban League	Nonprofit	$10,197,000	$4,780,896	$8,182,268
Curtis & Associates	For-profit	$35,805,000	n.a.	n.a.
Federation of Employment and Guidance Services (FEGS)	Nonprofit	$16,351,000	$71,653,883	$93,685,879
Goodwill Industries	Nonprofit	$49,397,715	$27,287,285	$39,386,149
Nonprofit Assistance Corp.	For-profit	$7,425,000	n.a.	n.a.
New York Association for New Americans	Nonprofit	$12,387,960	$21,019,557	$23,635,950
Research Foundation/ Bronx Community College	Nonprofit	$63,190,998	$165,474,232	$200,906,780
Wildcat Services Corporation	Nonprofit	$54,697,500	$8,066,836	$34,317,927

Source: Information on assets and income from www.Guidestar.org as of FY 2000.

n.a. = not applicable.

a. IMS was sold recently by Lockheed Martin to Affiliated Computer Services (ACS), a technology firm based in Dallas, Texas. ACS is a Fortune 1000 company that operates seventy-nine one-stops in fifty-nine contracts in thirty-six locations around the country. Because most of the contract activity analyzed here came before the merger, reference will be to Lockheed Martin IMS throughout.

b. Curtis & Associates was renamed Concera in 2002. In 1998, Benova, Inc., headquartered in Portland, Oregon, was acquired by AFSA Data Corporation, itself a wholly owned affiliate of FleetBoston Financial Corporation. Benova, Inc., acquired Curtis & Associates, headquartered in Kearney, Nebraska, in 2000. In 2002 Benova, Inc., Curtis & Associates, and the government contracting division of AFSA Data Corporation, headquartered in Long Beach, California, became the Concera Corporation. Concera specializes in contracting with federal, state, and local government agencies to provide a wide range of business process outsourcing solutions.

APPENDIX B

Individual Vendor Contracts

Table B-1. *MAXIMUS Direct-Service TANF/WIA Contracts, 2002*

Location	Contract term and value	Services provided
Arizona		
Arizona Works Pilot Project	4/1999–12/2002 $14,935,837	WIA registration; intake and eligibility determination; participant outreach/recruitment; orientation; assessment; individual responsibility plan; case management; resource center; pre-employment work skills; job search and life skills training; job placement; job retention services/follow-up; support services coordination; community outreach; employer outreach; on-site GED and ESL linkages; on-the-job training; career enhancement
California		
Orange County CalWORKs West	2000–02 $9,384,703	Case management; intake; appraisal; job readiness; job development; job placement; retention services; education; training employment supportive services
Orange County CalWORKs North	2000–02 $7,881,866	Orientation assessment; individual responsibility plan; case management; resource center; pre-employment work skills; job search and life skills; training placement; job retention/follow-up; support services coordination; community outreach

Table B-1. MAXIMUS Direct-Service TANF/WIA Contracts, 2002 (continued)

Location	Contract term and value	Services provided
Lake County CalWORKs	1999–2002 $2,100,000	Case management; assessments; orientation and appraisal; development of individual employment plans; supportive services arrangement; life skills workshops; job readiness training; job search activities; job development and job placement; and job follow-up
County of San Diego CalWORKs	2001–02 $9,384,703	Intake and assessment; case management; welfare to work individual plans; job placement; job development; job search; supportive services authorization; compliance monitoring and counseling
San Diego CalWORKs, South Bay Region	2/2001– 6/2002 $7,321,143	Orientation; assessment; individual responsibility plan; case management; resource center; pre-employment work skills; job search and life skills training; job placement; job retention services/follow-up; support services coordination; community outreach; employer outreach; on-site GED and ESL linkages; compliance monitoring; counseling
San Diego Refugee Services	7/2001– 6/2002 $357,323	For refugee recipients of TANF and Refugee Cash Assistance: orientation; assessment; individual responsibility plan; case management; resource center; pre-employment work skills; job search and life skills training; job placement; job retention services/follow-up; support services coordination; community outreach; employer outreach; on-site GED and ESL linkages; compliance monitoring; counseling
Delaware		
Delaware ABAWD	2001–02 $200,500	Participant outreach/recruitment; orientation; assessment; individual responsibility plan; case management; resource center; pre-employment work skills; job search and life skills training; job placement; job retention/follow-up; support services coordination; community outreach

continued on next page

Table B-1. *MAXIMUS Direct-Service TANF/WIA Contracts, 2002 (continued)*

Location	Contract term and value	Services provided
Delaware Keep A Job	10/2001– 9/2002 $213,875	Orientation; assessment; individual responsibility plan; intensive case management; resource center; pre-employment work skills; job search and life skills training; job placement; job retention services/follow-up; support services coordination; community outreach; employer outreach
District of Columbia		
District of Columbia	2000–01 $7,448,250	Participant outreach/recruitment; orientation; assessment; individual responsibility plan; case management; resource center; pre-employment work skills; job search and life skills training; job placement; job retention/follow-up; support services coordination; community outreach
Hawaii		
Aiea (Hawaii) Quick to Work Program	1999–2002 $405,357	Intake and assessment; orientation; case management; supportive services; client exit services; transitional health and child care; program transition planning
Waianae (Hawaii) First to Work	$405,357	Intake and assessment; orientation; case management; supportive services; client exit services; transitional health and child care; program transition planning
Illinois		
Chicago Workforce Development	4/2000– 6/2002 $2,378,213	WIA registration; intake and eligibility determination; participant outreach/recruitment; orientation; assessment; individual responsibility plan; case management; resource center; pre-employment work skills; job search and life skills training; job placement; job retention services/follow-up; support services coordination; community outreach; employer outreach

continued on next page

Table B-1. *MAXIMUS Direct-Service TANF/WIA Contracts, 2002 (continued)*

Location	Contract term and value	Services provided
Chicago Youth Empowerment	1/2001– 6/2002 $549,979	WIA registration; intake and eligibility determination; participant outreach/recruitment; orientation; assessment; individual responsibility plan; case management; resource center; pre-employment work skills; job search and life skills training; job placement; support services coordination; community outreach
Maryland		
Baltimore NCP	1999–2002 $795,227	Orientation/assessment; individual responsibility plan; case management; resource center; pre-employment work skills; job search and life skills training; job placement; job retention services/follow-up; support services coordination; community outreach
Montgomery County Employment Services Project	2000–02 $4,092,257	Assessment, job search, job readiness, life skills training, Employment Resource Center, coordination of supportive services, work experience, on-the-job training, job placement, referral to education and training programs, literacy, GED and computer work processing training
New York		
Albany WIA	2001–02 $700,000	WIA registration; intake and eligibility determination; participant outreach/recruitment; orientation; assessment; individual responsibility plan; case management; resource center; pre-employment work skills; job search and life skills training; job placement; job retention/follow-up; support services coordination; community outreach
Albany DSS	2000–02 $148,750	Orientation; assessment; individual responsibility plan; case management; resource center; pre-employment work skills; job search and life skills training; job placement; support services coordination; community outreach

continued on next page

Table B-1. *MAXIMUS Direct-Service TANF/WIA Contracts, 2002 (continued)*

Location	Contract term and value	Services provided
New York City Skills Assessment and Job Placement Project	1/2000– 2/2002 $4,022,245	Participant outreach/recruitment; orientation; assessment; individual responsibility plan; case management; resource center; pre-employment work skills; job search and life skills training; job placement; support services coordination; community outreach; employer outreach
New York State InVEST	12/2000– 2/2002 —	Orientation; assessment; individual responsibility plan; case management; resource center; pre-employment work skills; job search and life skills training; job placement; job retention services/follow-up; support services coordination; community outreach; employer outreach; vocational training
North Carolina		
North Carolina	2001–02 $700,000	Participant outreach/recruitment; orientation; assessment; individual responsibility plan; case management; resource center; pre-employment work skills; job search and life skills training; job placement; job retention/follow-up; support services coordination; community outreach
Charlotte/ Mecklenberg	2001–02 $391,200	Intake and eligibility determination; participant outreach/recruitment; orientation; assessment; individual responsibility plan; case management; resource center; pre-employment work skills; job search and life skills training; job placement; job retention services/follow-up; support services coordination; community outreach; employer outreach; on-site GED and ESL linkages; on-the-job training
New Jersey		
Work First New Jersey Special Employment Initiative Program	4/2001– 2/2002 —	Participant outreach/recruitment; engagement; reengagement
Wisconsin		
Wisconsin Works (W-2)	$28,127,571	Job readiness workshops; life skills workshops; retention workshops; job search; job development and placement; employment resource center; and job follow-up services

Table B-2. *MAXIMUS TANF Contracts That Have Ended*

Location	Contract term and value	Services provided
Los Angeles County GAIN Program	1988–93 $49,958,781	WIA registration; intake and eligibility determination; literacy; participant/outreach recruitment orientation; case management; intake; assessment; development of individualized employment plans; arrangement of supportive services; job readiness; job search training; job development and placement; retention services
El Paso JOBS	1998–99 $539,602	Orientation and appraisal; case management; motivationally focused job skills workshops; job development and placement; six months of follow-up services; and supportive services coordination
Virginia	1998–99 $1,681,973	Case management; orientation and appraisal; job readiness training; job search; job development and placement; retention for six months; and coordination of supportive services
Delaware Workfare	1996–99 $3,975,511	Case management; job readiness training; job search; client training and career development referral; job development and placement; and community work experience and full employment programs
Illinois Job Advantage Program	1998–2001 $4,779,000	Case management; intake and assessment; life skills; job search; Employment Resource Center; job development; job placement; 30-day retention follow-up; transportation plan development
Chicago Mayor's Office 155	1998–2000 $3,029,220	Assessment; case management; job readiness; job development; job placement; job retention; one-stop resource center; coordination of supportive services
Virginia Beach VIEW Program	1998–2000 $1,000,000	Skills appraisal and assessments; educational and vocational training referrals; job search and preparation workshops; job development and placement skills support and job coaching; work experience; workfare and internships; retention services
Pennsylvania Community Solutions Project	1999–2002 $2,352,167	Intake and eligibility determination; participant outreach/recruitment; orientation; assessment; individual responsibility plan; case management; resource center; pre-employment work skills; job search and life skills training; job placement; job retention/follow-up; support services coordination; community outreach

Table B-3. *Lockheed Martin TANF Client Service Contracts, 2001*

Location	Term (years)	Contract value	Current value	Contract type
California				
San Diego CalWORKs	4	$25,880,342	$8,412,195	GAIN
San Diego One Stop	1	$2,049,050	$2,049,050	WIA, TANF, WtW
District of Columbia				
District of Columbia	2	$9,838,250	$7,838,250	TANF
Florida				
WAGES Region 6: Hamilton, Jefferson, Lafayette, Madison, Suwannee, Taylor	1	$1,740,078	$1,740,078	WAGES, WIA
WAGES Region 7: Columbia, Dixie, Gilchrist, and Union	4	$4,026,372	$1,987,349	WAGES, WIA, WtW
WAGES Region 8 First Coast Jobs and Education Regional Board	2	$7,611,918	—	WAGES, WIA
WAGES Region 12: Central Florida Lake, Orange, Osceola, Seminole, and Sumter counties	4	$17,101,520	$6,998,626	WAGES, WIA
WAGES Region 14: The Pinellas WAGES Coalition	5	$10,815,818	$2,305,842	WAGES, WIA, WtW
WAGES Region 15: WAGES Coalition of Hillsborough County	1	$1,346,239	$1,346,239	WAGES
WAGES Region 17: Polk County Workforce Development Board	1	$940,581	$940,581	WAGES, WIA
WAGES Region 18: Sarasota and Manatee counties	2	$3,314,006	$1,578,039	WAGES, WIA, WtW
WAGES Region 21: Palm Beach County	5	$14,431,148	$2,380,000	WAGES, WIA, Eligibility Pilot
WAGES Region 22: Broward Employment & Training Admin. (BETA)	3	$7,263,692	$4,276,219	WAGES, WIA

continued on next page

Table B-3. *Lockheed Martin TANF Client Service Contracts, 2001 (continued)*

Location	Term (years)	Contract value	Current value	Contract type
WAGES Region 23: Miami-Dade & Monroe County Jobs & Education Partnership	2	$3,329,698	$1,732,962	WAGES, WIA
WAGES Region 23: Dade County	3	$2,400,000	$900,000	WAGES Intensive, WIA, WtW and Pre-sanction
WAGES Region 24: Collier, Lee, Charlotte, Hendry, and Glades counties	2	$3,223,662	$1,444,875	WAGES, WIA, WtW
Texas				
Cameron County Workforce Board	2	$8,878,892	$1,321,938	CHOICES, WIA, WtW, FS & ET
Capital Area Workforce Board	2	$6,968,715	$4,503,249	CHOICES, WIA, FS & ET
Concho Valley Workforce Board	1	$2,973,787	$2,973,787	CHOICES, WIA, WtW, FS & ET
Dallas County Workforce Board	1	$14,233,764	$14,233,764	CHOICES, WIA, WtW, FS & ET
Deep East Texas Work-force Development Board	1	$4,816,581	$4,816,581	CHOICES, WIA, WtW, FS & ET
East Texas Workforce Development Board	1	$3,199,317	$3,199,317	CHOICES, WIA, WtW, FS & ET
Gulf Coast Workforce Development Board	1	$9,064,696	$9,064,696	CHOICES, WIA, WtW, FS & ET
Heart of Texas Workforce Development Board	1	$9,064,696	$9,064,696	CHOICES, WIA, WtW, FS & ET
Lower Rio Grande Work-force Development Board	—	—	—	—
Upper Rio Grande Workforce	1	$16,721,746	$16,721,716	One-Stop, TANF, WIA, WtW, RRP
Rural Capital Area Work-force Development Board	2	—	$2,147,847	CHOICES, WIA, WtW, FS & ET
North East Texas Work-force Development Board	1	$9,122,979	$9,122,979	One Stop (WIA, CHOICES, WtW, FS & ET & CCMS)
Total	—	—	$108,212,905	—

Table B-4. *Lockheed Martin Non–TANF Based Contracts*

Location	Term (years)	Contract value	Current value	Contract type
California				
San Diego Refugee	4	$1,106,939	$305,259	Refugee employment
California ETP	1	$9,447,950	$9,447,950	ETP retention services
County of Los Angeles Department of Public Social Services	2	$13,829,872	—	GAIN
Michigan				
Wayne County Community Mental Health Agency	1	$1,996,730	$1,996,730	Wayne County special needs services MH-MR
Florida				
Abilities, Inc., of Florida	6 months	$799,984	$799,987	Vocational rehabilitation services
Texas				
Alamo Workforce Development, Inc.	1	$3,164,054	$3,164,054	DCA and Rapid Response Kelly base closing
East Texas Workforce Development Board	1	$5,159,292	$5,159,292	Child care services
Rural Capital Area Workforce Development Board	2	$1,600,000	$754,874	Child Care Management services
East Texas Council of Governments	1	$22,800	$22,800	Rural Expansion for One-Stop Centers
East Texas Council for Governments	1	$12,164,480	$12,164,480	Child Care Training
East Texas Council of Governments	1	$374,176	$374,176	NRA Grant
Total			$22,089,341	

Table B-5. *Curtis & Associates Direct-Service TANF Contracts, 2002*

Location	Contract term and value	Services provided
Arapaho Nation		
Arapaho Nation Social Services	10/15/99– 9/30/00 $89,315	Case manager training; workshop facilitator training; and assistance in establishing employment and training
California		
Santa Barbara: California Department of Social Services	09/93– 06/30/01 $1,686,243	Self-sufficiency center approach to case management system; appraisal; job-skills training; job-readiness and retention services for CalWORKs recipients
Kern County: Department of Human Services	07/98– 06/30/02 $5,500,111	Client service coordination (CSC) self-sufficiency center approach to case management and retention services for all CalWORKs participants
Orange County: California Department of Social Services	12/98– 12/31/01 $5,644,709	Job retention and employment support services to CalWORKs recipients
Ventura County: Human Service Agency	02/00– 09/30/02 $182,000	Life skills and job-retention workshops for WtW CalWORKs recipients and other JTPA participants
District of Columbia		
Department of Human Services	2000–02 $11,349,000	Skills assessment program involving orientation; job placement; job retention; and case management services
Florida		
Flagler and Volusia counties: Workforce Development Board	5/1/00– 6/30/02 $1,161,760	WAGES case management and job development
Indiana		
Hamilton County: Indiana Family and Social Services Administration	07/96– 09/30/02 $116,804	Performance-based job placement and job development for TANF and Food Stamp recipients

continued on next page

Table B-5. *Curtis & Associates Direct-Service TANF Contracts, 2002* *(continued)*

Location	Contract term and value	Services provided
Wayne County: Indiana Family and Social Services Administration	10/01/00– 09/30/02 $128,300	Performance-based job placement; job development; outreach; and assessment for TANF and Food Stamp recipients
Fayette County: State of Indiana Division of Family and Children	10/01/01– 9/30/02 —	Performance-based job placement; job development; and case management for TANF and Food Stamp recipients
Vanderburgh County: Indiana Family and Social Services Administration	07/96– 09/30/02 $175,670	Performance-based job placement; job development; and case management for TANF and Food Stamp recipients
Maryland		
Mayor's Office of Employment Development, City of Baltimore, Baltimore Workforce Investment Board	11/1/01– 6/30/03 —	Operate One-Stop Career Center to assist individuals in obtaining and retaining employment; services including assessments, access to Maryland Job Bank, Internet access, job readiness, workshops, and job placement
Michigan		
Detroit Employment and Training	04/95– 09/30/01 $757,926	A Work-First program involving case management, job-seeking skills training, and postemployment workshops
Nebraska		
Nebraska Department of Health and Human Service, Northern Service Area	05/95–8/02 —	Full case management; job readiness/life skills; job seeking and employment retention workshops; education planning; monitoring; work experience; on-the-job training; and micro-business
Nebraska Department of Health and Human Service, Southwest Service Area	05/85–06/02 —	Full case management; job readiness/life skills; job seeking and employment retention workshops; education planning; monitoring; work experience; on-the-job training; and micro-business

continued on next page

Table B-5. *Curtis & Associates Direct-Service TANF Contracts, 2002 (continued)*

Location	Contract term and value	Services provided
Nebraska Department of Health and Human Service, Northern Service Area	05/85–06/02 —	Full case management; job readiness/life skills; job seeking and employment retention workshops; education planning; monitoring
Nebraska Department of Labor, Central Service Area	05/95– 06/30/04 $2,449,224	Job readiness/life management skills; job-seeking skills; and employment retention skills and individual coaching; and education planning and monitoring. Serves cash assistance and Food Stamp recipients
New York		
City of New York, Human Resources Administration/FIA	12/99– 11/30/02 $8,977,500	Skills assessment program involving orientation, job placement, job retention, and case management services
City of New York, Human Resources Administration/FIA	12/99– 11/30/02 $11,935,000	Employment services/placement program involving job placement and job retention activities
North Carolina		
Mecklenberg County Department of Social Services	07/99– 06/30/02 $954,819	Case management services
Capital Area Workforce Development Board, Wake County, N.C.	02/99– 1/30/01 $370,000	Recruitment, job readiness, job search, community outreach, and job retention services for Welfare-to-Work program targeting noncustodial parents and individuals whose TANF time limits have expired
North Dakota		
Department of Social Services	07/95– 09/30/02 $316,785	Job-seeking skills workshops, monitoring of job-search activity and work experience for Food Stamp/ABAWD recipients
Ohio		
Board of Commissioners of Montgomery County, Department of Human Services	03/1/00– 2002 —	Work opportunity program offering orientations, peer support groups, job-search, life management skills and workplace skills workshops, and case management

continued on next page

Table B-5. *Curtis & Associates Direct-Service TANF Contracts, 2002 (continued)*

Location	Contract term and value	Services provided
Clermont County Department of Human Services/Ohio Works First	10/97–2002 —	Performance-based employment counseling services consisting of case management, self-assessment, job-search workshops, job placement, work experience, and job retention services
Clermont County Department of Human Services/Ohio Works First	10/00–1/02 —	One-stop operator
Clermont County Department of Human Services/Ohio Works First	10/00–1/02 —	WIA administrator
Montgomery County: Ohio Department of Human Services	07/95– 12/31/01 $250,000	Performance-based job placement and job development for TANF and Food Stamp recipients
Pennsylvania		
Allegheny County, Commonwealth of Pennsylvania, Department of Public Welfare, Bureau of Employment and Training Programs	06/01–05/02 —	Service to connect TANF clients who currently have little or no employment, training or educational activities, through the Community Connections Initiative Grants program
State of Pennsylvania, Bureau of Employment	03/00– 02/28/04 $223,960	Rapid Re-Employment Program involving job-seeking skills workshops and monitoring of job-search activities for TANF recipients in the City of Philadelphia
Wisconsin		
State of Wisconsin, Department of Work-force Development in Waukesha	10/97–12/01 $1,582,219	Overseeing W-2, Food Stamps, Medical Assistance, and Childcare Eligibility, and providing services to W-2 employment, Food Stamp employment, and training participants

continued on next page

Table B-5. *Curtis & Associates Direct-Service TANF Contracts, 2002*
(continued)

Location	Contract term and value	Services provided
Sheboygan County: Wisconsin Department of Social Services	07/89–12/31/02 $154,219	Job-seeking skills and life skills workshops for TANF-eligible participants and job center customers; mentoring of job seeking and personal enhancement activities; community service jobs; W-2 transition jobs; trial jobs and work experiences. Development and coordination for W-2 and Food Stamp recipients; children first program for noncustodial parents; and job center integration services for collaboration of six agencies
Wyoming Wyoming Department of Family Services	07/89–06/30/02 $597,000	Case management, including job-search workshops, recruitment, employer contacts, and job readiness programs for TANF recipients

Table B-6. *Curtis & Associates Indirect-Service TANF Contracts, 2002*

Location	Contract term and value	Services provided
Arizona		
Department of Economic Security/ JOBS Administration	03/97– 6/30/02 $1,029,000	Develop curriculum and train providers for employment preparation of TANF recipients
California		
San Mateo: California Department of Social Services	04/94– 06/30/02 $50,000	Job-search consulting
Alameda County: California Department of Social Services	07/96– 06/30/00 $50,000	Job-search consulting training
Tulare County: Health and Human Services Agency	01/98– 06/30/01 $53,000	Job-search consultant training
City and County of San Francisco: California Department of Social Services	10/95– 06/30/02 $57,000	Job-search consultant training
Clermont County Department of Human Services	07/00– 06/30/01 $180,000	Front-line supervisor training
Board of County Commissioners of Clermont County, Clermont County Department of Human Services	02/10/00– 06/30/01 $261,120	Bridges pilot program to provide engagement, pre-employment training, retention, and monitoring services to felony non-support, noncustodial parents and post-release incarcerated offenders who fall at the 200-percent poverty level or below

Table B-7. *Curtis & Associates Expired TANF Contracts, 2002*

Location	Contract term and value	Services provided
State of Wisconsin	1996–12/31/ 99 (ended) $43,250	Training development and facilitation of state and federal policy to front-line workers and management in the areas of W-2 (TANF), Food Stamp Employment and Training (FSET), childcare, job retention and interpersonal topical areas; technical assistance on program policy and CARES
New York State Department of Labor	8/98–8/31/00 (ended) $107,653	Employment Agency Initiative job placement and job-retention services for TANF recipients
Opportunity America- New York City	9/98–9/30/99 (ended) $162,378	In partnership with Opportunity America, recruits people receiving public assistance, design integrated curriculum, implement Retail Skills training, recruit businesses to interview and hire, and follow-up services ensuring job retention
KAISER Group, Inc.	8/98–12/31/99 (ended) $323,850	Orientation and job search consulting for the Kaiser Organization, which is contracted with the Human Resources Administration of New York City
Opportunity America-West- chester, New York	4/98–12/31/99 (ended) $387,943	A subcontractor to Opportunity America, provides interactive job search workshops for 3,000 people
City of New York, Human Resources Administration/FIA	8/98–7/1/99 (ended) $700,000	Welfare to work involving Resource Rooms at HRA's Job Centers. Provide job search skills, job placement, and job retention skills
City of New York, Human Resources Administration/FIA	7/95–10/29/99 (ended) $1,310,512	Operation of Employment Centers, which include job-search and job readiness workshops for Home Relief recipients
Family Support Services Division, Department of Human Services, Oklahoma City, OK	5/98–6/30/00 (ended) $278,104	Employment-focused case management including orientation, assessment, employ- ment planning, pre-employment workshops, and one-year post-employment job retention coaching
Private Industry Council of Philadelphia, Incorporated	4/99–12/31/99 (ended) $405,554	Directed Job Search program involving intensive job placement for job ready participants who have received cash welfare assistance for twenty-four months or more

continued on next page

Table B-7. *Curtis & Associates Expired TANF Contracts, 2002 (continued)*

Location	Contract term and value	Services provided
Kansas Department of Social and Rehabilitation Services, Emporia SRS Area	6/98–6/30/00 (ended) $1,557,303	Employment and retention services. Orientation, assessment, job search/life management skills (group and individual), coordination of services for individuals including those with disabilities and barriers
San Joaquin County, California Human Services Agency	01/99–12/31/00 $6,257,401	Self-sufficiency center approach to case management and retention
Bartholomew County, Indiana Family and Social Services Administration	07/97–09/30/00 $125,676	Performance-based job placement, job development, job coaching, and job retention for TANF and Food Stamp recipients
Knox County, Indiana Family and Social Services Administration	10/01/99- 09/30/00 $212,250	Performance-based job placement, job development, job retention, assessment, and outreach for TANF and Food Stamp recipients
Marion County, Indiana Family and Social Services Administration	07/95–09/30/00 $176,000	Performance-based job placement, job development, and job retention for TANF and Food Stamp recipients
Board of County Commissioners of Montgomery County (Md.), Montgomery County Department of Human Services	03/01/00– 06/30/01 $185,000	Seek Work Opportunity Program offering orientations, peer support groups, job-search, life management skills and workplace skills workshops, and case management
City of New York, Human Resources Administration/ Welfare to Work	02/98–09/30/00 $618,250	Job retention services
Philadelphia Workforce Development Corporation	07/01/00– 01/31/01 $661,000	Directed Job Search program involving intensive job placement for job-ready participants who have received cash welfare assistance for twenty-four months or more

continued on next page

Table B-7. *Curtis & Associates Expired TANF Contracts, 2002 (continued)*

Location	Contract term and value	Services provided
City of Philadelphia, Department of Public Welfare	11/01/99– 10/31/00 $639,000	Job retention, advancement, and rapid re-employment. Computer basic skills training, CAN training, retention, support services, and assistance to first-time home buyers. Curtis & Associates, Inc., contributes to family savings plans, which helps home buyers attend class for the down payment of their first homes
Private Industry Council of Milwaukee County, Inc.	03/99–02/28/01 $412,500	Employment maintenance organization to provide Welfare-to-Work eligible, non-custodial parents with community service employment, recruitment, engagement, pre-employment training, case management, retention and monitoring services

Sources: For MAXIMUS: Akbar Piloti, MAXIMUS executive vice president, Welfare Reform Division; and Judye Yellon, MAXIMUS vice president, Workforce Services. For Lockheed Martin IMS: Dr. Amy Zeitler, business development manager; and Tom Scott, contracts/compliance manager. For Curtis & Associates, www.selfsufficiency.com/index.html.

Notes

Chapter 1

1. Barbara Bezdek, "Contractual Welfare: Non-Accountability and Diminished Democracy in Local Government Contracts for Welfare-to-Work Service," *Fordham Urban Law Journal*, June 2001, vol. 17, Rev. 1559.

2. Even these service areas, however, have experienced increasing attention for privatization. See Elliot D. Sclar, *You Don't Always Get What You Pay For: The Economics of Privatization* (Cornell University Press, 2000).

3. As of 1998, more than thirty states had turned over parts of their welfare systems to private contractors. In many localities this trend has accelerated over the past two years. Richard Wolf, "Public Aid Going Private in Many States," *USA Today*, August 3, 1998, p. 3A. In a 2002 survey on government contracting of TANF services, the Government Accounting Office (GAO) reported that all states with the exception of North Dakota and including the District of Columbia have contracted for TANF-funded services. At the state level, contracting occurs in twenty-four states, only at the local level in five, and at both in the remaining twenty states, as well as in the District of Columbia. "Welfare Reform: Interim Report on Potential Ways to Strengthen Federal Oversight of State and Local Contracting," GAO-02-245, April 23, 2002.

4. Peter Frumkin and Alice Andre-Clark, "When Missions, Markets and Politics Collide: Values and Strategy in the Non-Profit Human Services," *Non-Profit and Voluntary Sector Quarterly*, vol. 29, no.1, supplement 2000, pp. 141–63.

5. Recent proposals for the reauthorization legislation due in 2003 seek to increase the mandate to 70 percent.

6. A recent GAO survey found that as a result of the changing environment induced in part by both PRWORA and the Workforce Investment Act (WIA), the extent of contracting, especially with the private sector, is dramatically changed. GAO, "Welfare Reform," GAO-02-245, p. 6.

7. Ibid.

8. The U.S. General Accounting Office recently completed a survey of all fifty states and ten counties with the largest federal TANF funding allocations in the thirteen states that administer welfare locally. Ibid.

9. While in no site studied were contractors actually competing head to head for clients, multiple contractors in a single jurisdiction are inevitably in competition since their performance is systematically compared and future contract renewals are likely to be based on comparative performance. The study's sample is not representative. Two types of settings were excluded: jurisdictions where a single contractor dominated the market and jurisdictions that relied primarily on community colleges. Many sites using a single contractor had engaged for-profit providers, but their virtual monopoly did not permit the interactive effects across the sectors studied. Further, in many smaller jurisdictions the principal providers are community colleges. In only one of the sites, New York City, was one of the contractors a community college. There, the mix of providers included for-profits and nonprofits of various types. The relative impact of community colleges is an important dimension not included in this study. See Alexandra de Montrichard and Edwin Melendez, "Welfare to Work Initiative in California and Los Angeles," unpublished paper, Mauricio Gaston Institute, University of Massachusetts, Boston, Mass.; and Lynn McCormick, "Community Colleges in New York's Welfare Setting," unpublished paper, Hunter College, New York, N.Y.

10. Recently, the GAO included all these sites in its case studies as well, because they represent jurisdictions with large TANF allocations and significant contracting out to private vendors of welfare-to-work activities.

11. Donald F. Kettl, *Sharing Power* (Brookings, 1993), p. 19.

Chapter 2

1. Accountability is herein defined as preserving the "public trust" through assuming responsibility for resources, outcomes, and processes (including fairness and democratic process). For an excellent discussion see Robert D. Behn, *Rethinking Democratic Accountability* (Brookings, 2001).

2. Donald F. Kettl, *Sharing Power: Public Governance and Private Markets* (Brookings, 1993), p. 13.

3. Ibid.

4. At this writing, daily revelations about corporate greed and fraud following the Enron revelations dominate the media. Whether these scandals will cool the current enthusiasm for private market service solutions is worth monitoring.

5. New York City, for example, has contracted with sectarian philanthropic organizations for the provision of social services for more than one hundred years. See James Krauskopf, "Privatization of Human Services in New York City: Some Examples and Lessons," paper presented at the Annual Research Conference of the Association for Public Policy Analysis and Management, October, 1995. Based on work supported by the Twentieth Century Fund. See

also Steven Rathgeb Smith and Michael Lipsky, *Nonprofits for Hire: The Welfare State in the Age of Contracting* (Harvard University Press, 1993).

6. Mark Hoover, formerly executive deputy administrator, NYC Human Resources Administration, interview with author, June 29, 2000.

7. See, in particular, Virginia Hodgkinson, "Assessing the Role of the Non-Profit Sector Following Welfare Reform: What Do We Know? What Do We Need to Know?" Working Paper, Georgetown Public Policy Institute, February 2000.

8. Kent Weaver, *Ending Welfare as We Know It* (Brookings, 2000).

9. Margaret Gibelman, "Theory, Practice, and Experience in the Purchase of Services," in Margaret Gibelman and Harold W. Demone Jr., eds., *The Privatization of Human Services* (Springer, 1998), pp. 1–51. See also C. T. Cruthirds, "The Community Action Program Agency and Voluntary Delegate Organizations: Issues in Interorganizational Contracting," Ph.D. dissertation, Tulane University, New Orleans, La., 1972; K. R. Wendel, "Government Contracting for Purchase of Service," *Social Work,* vol. 21 (1976), pp. 101–05; R. M. Kramer, "An Analysis of Policy Issues in Relationships between Government and Voluntary Social Welfare Agencies," Ph.D. dissertation, University of California, Berkeley, 1964; M. Gibelman and H. W. Demone, "The Evolving Contract State," in H. W. Demone and M. Gibelman, eds., *Services for Sale: Purchasing Health and Human Services* (Rutgers University Press, 1989) pp. 17–57.

10. Linda M. Lampkin and Thomas H. Pollack, *The New Nonprofit Almanac and Desk Reference: The Essential Facts and Figures for Managers, Researchers, and Volunteers* (Urban Institute, 2002), pp. 100–01.

11. Donald F. Kettl, *The Global Public Management Revolution: A Report on the Transformation of Governance* (Brookings, 2000), p. 69.

12. Lester M. Salamon, *Partners in Public Service: Government-Nonprofit Relations in the Modern Welfare State* (Johns Hopkins University Press, 1995).

13. Smith and Lipsky, *Nonprofits for Hire,* p. 21.

14. Ibid., p. 22.

15. Ibid.

16. Mancur Olson, *The Logic of Collective Action* (Harvard University Press, 1965).

17. Lampkin and Pollack, *The New Nonprofit Almanac,* pp. 100–01.

18. U.S. General Accounting Office (GAO), "Welfare Reform: Interim Report on Potential Ways to Strengthen the Federal Oversight of State and Local Contracting," GAO-02-245, April 2002, pp. 26–31.

19. Lester Salamon, "Rethinking Public Management: Third Party Government and the Changing Forms of Government Action," *Public Policy,* vol. 29, no. 3 (Summer 1981), pp. 255–75; and Salamon, *Partners in Public Service,* p. 187.

20. Lester Salamon, ed., *Beyond Privatization: The Tools of Government Action* (Urban Institute, 1989), pp. 8–9.

21. Martin Minogue, Charles Polidano, and David Hume, eds., *Beyond the New Public Management: Changing Ideas and Practices in Governance* (Northampton, Mass.: Edward Elgar, 1998), p. xv.

22. Kettl, *The Global Public Management Revolution,* p. 6.

23. Ibid., p. 27.

24. Six core characteristics of new public management reform efforts as described by Kettl are: productivity, marketization, service orientation, decentralization, policy, and accountability for results. Ibid.

25. Ibid., p. 3.

26. Martin Levin and Mary Bryna Sanger, *Making Government Work* (Jossey-Bass, 1994); Robert Behn, *Leadership Counts* (Harvard University Press, 1991).

27. In all these cases public employees unions resisted the reforms. In one high-profile case, the governor of Connecticut ultimately rescinded his technology outsourcing initiative, deciding instead to use state employees to modernize with more selective contracting. Similarly, to quell dissent but sustain their innovations, the San Diego Board of Supervisors protected public jobs by requiring vendors to offer employment to all "in-scope" employees and sustain their salaries and fringe benefits for at least 150 days.

28. William B. Eimicke, "San Diego County's Innovation Program: Using Competition and a Whole Lot More to Improve Public Service," grant report, PricewaterhouseCoopers Endowment for the Business of Government, January 2000.

29. Lockheed Martin recently sold its IMS division to a Dallas-based company, Affiliated Computer Services. ACS is a Fortune 1000 company that now operates seventy one-stop centers in thirty-six locations and employs 30,000 people. Its net income for the six months ending December 2001, including the IMS acquisition, was $99.5 million, a 59 percent increase over the previous year. See ACS press release, PRNewswire, January 22, 2002.

30. All states are now mandated by the federal government to have electronic benefit transfers for Food Stamp recipients by 2001. Citicorp is currently the largest contractor in this area.

31. Robert D. Behn and Peter Kant, "Strategies for Avoiding the Pitfalls of Performance Contracting," *Public Productivity and Management Review*, vol. 22, no. 4 (June 1999), pp. 470–89.

32. GAO, "Welfare Reform," GAO-02-245, pp. 18–19.

33. There are exceptions, however. The city has given approximately three months' advances of expected performance payments to keep contractors afloat as they make client investments but wait to demonstrate placement success and retention.

34. Alleging that the mayor's office used a questionable bidding process to quickly select favored contractors, and that MAXIMUS officials had been given improper access to information before the release of the bids, New York City comptroller Allen Hevesi attempted to block the $104 million contract from going forward (*Giuliani* v. *Hevisi*). The mayor filed suit in March of 2000, lost, then appealed. On appeal, the Appellate Division of State Supreme Court ruled in favor of the mayor. According to the decision, Hevesi had no right under the city charter to prevent the contracts from going forward. Hevesi dropped the ten-month dispute, but MAXIMUS is still not up and running in New York City. Eric Lipton, "Hevesi Quietly Drops 10-Month Fight to Block Welfare-to-Work

Contracts," *New York Times*, December 2, 2000. According to MAXIMUS spokeswoman Rachel Roland, they intend to work under a much smaller contract of $3 million, though the contracts have yet to be spent down. The Bloomberg administration recently made it clear it intended to allow the MAXIMUS contracts to lapse when they expire at the end of December 2002, and it did. See Michael Cooper, "Giuliani Fought Hard for Job Placement Work," *New York Times*, October 4, 2002, p. B1.

35. Richard Bonamarte, executive vice president, Wildcat Services Corporation, interview with author, January 25, 2001. Bonamarte was formerly the New York City chief procurement officer, Mayor's Office of Contracts, and executive deputy administrator for contracts and procurement at HRA.

36. Ibid.

37. Ibid.

38. John D. Donahue, *The Privatization Decision: Public Ends, Private Means* (Basic Books, 1989), pp. 179–211.

39. Kettl, *Sharing Power*.

40. William B. Eimicke, "San Diego County's Innovation Program," p. 13.

41. The decline in the attractiveness of government public service is well documented with the declining confidence the public has in government performance. Interviews confirmed that bureaucratic constraints on performance and innovation provide a high degree of frustration for public servants. The opportunity to provide similar services in more hospitable (and often better compensated) environments is a big draw. See Andrew Kohut, *Deconstructing Distrust: How Americans View Government* (Washington: The Pew Research Center, March 1998); and Paul Light, *The New Public Service* (Brookings, 1999).

42. Five organizations have conducted two to four similar studies over the past fifteen years: the U.S. Bureau of the Census, National Association of Counties (NAC), the International City/County Management Association (ICMA), the Mercer Group, Inc., and the Council of State Governments (CSG). See also Florencio Lopez-de-Silane and others, "Privatization in the United States," Working Paper 5113 (Cambridge, Mass.: National Bureau of Economic Research, May 1995).

43. Mildred E. Warner and Robert Hebdon, "Local Government Restructuring: Privatization and Its Alternatives," *Journal of Policy Analysis and Management,* vol. 20, no. 2 (Spring 2001).

44. Among the range of restructuring alternatives they report are: privatization, mixed public/private provision, cooperation between governments, and internal management improvements. See Mildred Warner and Amir Hefetz, "Privatization and the Market Restructuring Role of Local Government," paper presented at the Economic Policy Institute Conference on Privatization, Washington, January 11, 2000.

45. Smith and Lipsky, *Nonprofits for Hire,* p. 5.

46. U.S. Bureau of the Census, "Service Annual Survey: 1996" (Washington, 1998), pp. 93–103.

47. W. P. Ryan, "Background, Research and Opinion: For Profit Human Service Providers," unpublished manuscript, Pew Charitable Trusts, 1997, quoted in Peter Frumkin and Alice Andre-Clark, "When Missions, Market and Politics

Collide: Values and Strategy in the Nonprofit Human Services," *Nonprofit and Voluntary Sector Quarterly*, vol. 29, no.1 (Supplement 2000), p. 145.

48. These are state maintenance-of-effort funds that represent the mandated portion of the state's share.

49. Contracting occurs only at the state level in twenty-four states, only at the local level in five states, and at both levels in the remaining twenty states and the District of Columbia. GAO, "Welfare Reform," GAO-02-245, p. 8.

50. Ibid., pp. 12–13.

51. These include Lockheed Martin IMS (now Affiliated Computer Services, Inc.), MAXIMUS, America Works, Curtis and Associates, and ARBOR, Inc., to name a few. See table 1-1.

Chapter 3

1. A good summary list can be found in Margaret Gibelman, "Theory, Practice, and Experience in the Purchase of Services," in Margaret Gibelman and Harold W. Demone Jr., eds., *The Privatization of Human Services* (Springer, 1998). See also Sheila Kamerman and Alfred Kahn, *Privatization, Contracting, and Reform of Child and Family Social Services* (Washington: The Finance Project, 1998).

2. Other cities are experiencing similar shifts in service providers that are increasingly private. Chicago is a good example. See Evelyn Z. Brodkin and others, "Contracting Welfare Reform: Uncertainties of Capacity Building within Disjointed Federalism," unpublished paper, University of Chicago. For results of a fifty-state survey on contracting for welfare to work, see also U.S. General Accounting Office (GAO), "Welfare Reform: Interim Report on the Potential Ways to Strengthen Federal Oversight of State and Local Contracting," GAO-02-245, April 2002.

3. In Wyoming and Hawaii, 100 percent of contracted funds went to private for-profit contractors. GAO, "Welfare Reform," GAO-02-245.

4. Future researchers seeking more empirically based conclusions about the role of competition as distinct from the contribution of private provision in costs and outcomes would be advised to include cases where sole-source providers were selected. I was more interested in the relative effects of competition on each type of provider. Thus I wanted jurisdictions with a mix.

5. These were two separate sets of contracts with two different requests for proposals. Assessment and direct job placement resulted in five contracts of $103.3 million. Job training and placement resulted in eleven contracts of $302.6 million, including the MAXIMUS contract at a level greatly reduced from its original award. Contract information retrieved from the New York Office of Contracts' Vendex system. Information regarding the reduced level of the MAXIMUS award provided by Rachel Rowland, MAXIMUS spokesperson.

6. Milwaukee ultimately became a model of sorts for New York City.

7. In its most recent round of contract renewals, Employment Solutions, Inc., a subsidiary of Goodwill, dropped out after disputes about the appropriateness of some of its spending, which was uncovered in a state legislative audit. Its region was subsequently divided up among the remaining contractors.

8. The contract awarded to the public organization, Gulfcoast Careers of Harris County, was recently discontinued because of problems with its accounting system. Information provided by Mike Temple, Houston Galveston Area Council.

9. A growing literature exists assessing the virtues and pitfalls of privatization and contracting out for public and human services. See, for example, Ruth H. DeHoog, *Contracting Out for Human Services: Economic, Political and Organizational Perspectives* (State University of New York Press, 1984); Donald F. Kettl, *Sharing Power* (Brookings, 1993); E. S. Savas, *Privatization: The Key to Better Government* (Chatham House, 1987); E. S. Savas, *Privatization and Public-Private Partnerships* (Chatham House, 2000); John D. Donahue, *The Privatization Decision: Public Ends, Private Means* (Basic Books, 1989); Sheila Kamerman and Alfred Kahn, *Privatization and the Welfare State* (Princeton University Press, 1989); Elliot D. Sclar, *You Don't Always Get What You Pay For: The Economics of Privatization* (Cornell University Press, 2000); Lester Salamon, *Partners in Public Service: Government-Nonprofit Relations in the Modern Welfare State* (Johns Hopkins University Press, 1995); Lester Salamon, ed., *Beyond Privatization: The Tools of Government Action* (Urban Institute, 1989).

10. This, of course, will be the strategy under the new WIA legislation, where customer choice of qualified providers will dictate vendors' caseloads. Unlike the client referrals made by geographic location for TANF cases, WIA providers will need to compete for enrollment of clients.

11. This is an eventuality under the new WIA program, in which vendors will be "qualified" and then will compete to attract clients, being paid only when employment has been achieved. In Houston, where contractors serve both TANF and WIA clients, they have a slight incentive to recruit successful TANF clients after they have been initially enrolled in another contractor's program.

12. Other jurisdictions have experimented with a single for-profit contractor with mixed results, especially in Texas and Florida, where Lockheed Martin IMS dominates the welfare employment market. Los Angeles had an exclusive contract with MAXIMUS as well (1989–93), but reverted under change in administrations (and politics) to public provision until recently, when the county system was turned over to two for-profit providers, MAXIMUS and Lockheed Martin IMS. According to the April 2002 GAO report "Welfare Reform," the county is now providing services in addition to the for-profits, also with mixed results. GAO-02-245, p. 36.

13. Private contractors in all the cities expressed the view that there was a bias against them that necessitated a continual sensitivity to public relations. One articulate reporter on this was Jerry Stepaniak, vice president of Welfare Reform Division, MAXIMUS, and project director of the Milwaukee site. Interview with author April 25, 2001.

14. Information provided by Welfare Policy Center, Hudson Institute, State Plans Summary, www.acf.dhhs.gov/programs/ofa/PROVIS.HTM.

15. Data provided by Diane Francis, assistant director of Calworks, San Diego County Department of Health and Human Services.

16. These programs were designed at a time when overall employment rates were high and economic expansion had continued unabated for six years. Economic expansion began and the recession ended in 1991. Employment growth began the following year. National Bureau of Economic Research, www.nber.org/march91.html.

17. Data provided by Swati Desai, acting executive deputy administrator, Human Resources Administration.

18. While the process was more flexible and gave city administrators more discretion as to who was selected and the specific design of each contract, advocates and good government groups lobbied against the lack of openness and reduced opportunities for public scrutiny. See Tracie McMillan, "The Great Training Robbery," *City Limits*, May 2001.

19. Controversy surrounding the MAXIMUS contract alone precipitated a series of lawsuits brought by the New York City comptroller in 2000, which took seven months to resolve. See chapter 2, note 34.

20. In retrospect, this was found to be unnecessary. While caseloads declined dramatically in all sites, costs and service needs did not. The increasing needs of more disadvantaged caseloads continue to place significant demands on the systems. Indeed, the contract renewals in Milwaukee provided levels of funding similar to the early contracts, declining by only 20 percent in a four-year period, even though the number of clients expected to be served had declined significantly due to time limits and expected placement rates. Similar trends are found in New York City and San Diego. According to Diana Francis, assistant director of CalWORKs in San Diego, caseloads have declined by almost one-third, but contract awards have not. They are working on developing a system that can track caseloads better in order to assess how they will affect contracts in the future, as there are mixed responses on whether the remaining clients require more intensive services.

21. Although New York and Milwaukee had previously used CBOs and other employment and training contractors to provide job search and placement services to welfare clients under the JOBS program or who were receiving welfare-to-work services under JTPA, the scale of engagement necessitated by the new TANF legislation made traditional contracts totally inadequate. The new expectations necessitated a different consideration of the size of contracts and the number and capacity of providers.

22. Mark Hoover, first deputy commissioner of the New York City Human Resources Administration; interview with author, June 29, 2000.

23. George Leutermann, vice president for Welfare Reform Division; interview with author, January 13, 2000. Leutermann was formerly a Goodwill executive and administrator in child protection in Milwaukee; he later held a number of positions in the Wisconsin W-2 welfare reform effort. Some of his major accomplishments in these areas include large-scale outsourcing and privatization efforts.

24. Joan Zinser, deputy director, County of San Diego Health and Human Services Agency; interview with author, July 19, 2000.

25. Milwaukee's first round of contracts, instead of being performance based, simply allowed contractors to retain cost savings from delivering services more cheaply than the contracted amount. This kind of incentive can result in windfalls to contractors should they choose to reduce services rather than manage them efficiently. The second round restructured the contracts on a performance basis and capped potential profits.

26. An informal focus group with TANF clients and interviews with administrators of a Houston CBO, Houston Read Commission, revealed consistent complaints about understaffing and undertrained staff at the career centers, a result that was explained by a subtle effort to discourage clients from using costly services.

27. See table 1-1 for contract payment characteristics.

28. Interview with author, April 24, 2001.

29. See GAO, "Welfare Reform," GAO-02-245, pp. 31–36.

30. Data provided by the Executive Deputy Administrator for Policy, New York City Human Resources Administration PA Summary Report, ESP EmploymentVendor*Stat Report (October 2001), p. 136, n. 30.

31. GAO, "Welfare Reform," GAO-02-245.

32. Bob Kornfield, "Evaluation of the Arizona Works Pilot Program; Second Impact Study Report," Abt Associates, Cambridge, Mass., February 2002.

33. The GAO found an abundance of accountability lapses in virtually every site its representatives visited. GAO, "Welfare Reform," GAO-02-245, pp. 20–30.

34. Information from the New York City Comptroller's Office of Contracts confirmed that HRA is often six or more months behind in paying contractors, in large part due to its difficulty in verifying placements and other contract monitoring functions. Most often, auditing is done post hoc, making it impossible to ensure compliance with contract terms.

35. Frances Abbadessa, executive deputy for finance, New York City Human Resources Administration; interview with author, January 8, 2002.

36. GAO, "Welfare Reform," GAO-02-245, pp. 28–29.

37. David Heaney, project director for MAXIMUS in San Diego; interview with author, October 30, 2000.

38. MAXIMUS originally had more, with contracts of $104 million, but the two MAXIMUS contracts were held up in the courts for more than seven months after the New York City comptroller rejected them on the basis of significant fraud in the company's access to and role in the bidding process. The process differed from a typical competitive bidding process in reducing the city's requirements to open the process to any bidder and avoiding a rigid standard by which winners were chosen. This "negotiated acquisition process" has created significant and ongoing backlash from advocates and historical providers for the same reasons that the city used it: to speed up the process, reduce red tape, and avoid the political advocacy that normally takes place. The process as a consequence was less open, encouraged bidding by fewer contractors, and permitted the city considerably more discretion and secrecy.

39. Dick Buschmann, administrator for the Financial Assistance Division of the Milwaukee County Department of Human Services; interview with author, April 24, 2001.

40. Mike Johnson, "County Workers Get Key W-2 Role: $5 Million Contract to Provide for Initial Assessment of Clients," *Milwaukee Journal Sentinel*, p. 3B, September 19, 2001.

41. Kettl, *Sharing Power*, p. 19.

42. San Diego has conflicting political objectives that may be driving its administrative practices. Two county regions are currently being served by the county Health and Human Services Agency. Ensuring their competitive viability while trying to create a level playing field may have induced the county to impose many of the same bureaucratic requirements on private contractors that it imposes on the county agency.

43. Robert D. Behn and Peter Kant, "Strategies for Avoiding the Pitfalls of Performance Contracting," *Public Productivity Review*, vol. 22, no. 4 (June 1999), pp. 470–89.

44. New York, like Milwaukee, caps profits of for-profit firms at 15 percent, and there is a requirement for a 5 percent reinvestment in program activities. Nonprofits are limited to a 15 percent increase in program income as well. Vendors are required to report all cash flow, including profits and administrative expenses, so that the agency can track these caps.

45. Joan Zinser, deputy director, County of San Diego Health and Human Services Agency; interview with author, July 19, 2000.

46. Mark Hoover, First Deputy Commissioner of the New York City Human Resources Administration; interview with author, June 29, 2000.

47. This included privatizing the solid waste system, a bonus program for top managers, outsourcing of information technology and telecommunications services, and the use of a competition and reengineering group to speed the use of competition, lower costs, and improve customer service across agencies. These innovations were part of an overall strategy to avert bankruptcy threatening the county in 1995. See William B. Eimicke, "San Diego County's Innovation Program: Using Competition and a Whole Lot More to Improve Public Services," grant report, PricewaterhouseCoopers Endowment for the Business of Government, January 2000.

48. The original contracts totaled $104 million for Skills Assessment and Job Placement (SAP) and Employment Services and Job Placement (ESP). Current amounts for the three-year period are now allocated at a total of $3 million for both contracts. When they expired in December 2002 they were not renewed. See Michael Cooper, "Disputed Pacts for Welfare Will Just Die," *New York Times*, October 4, 2002, p. B1.

49. Lisa Greene, "County Sued over Lockheed Contract," *St. Petersburg Times*, Tuesday, January 8, 2002; *Largo Times*, p. 1.

Chapter 4

1. Paul Light, *The New Public Service* (Brookings, 1999).

2. Some of the most important nationally are Goodwill, the YWCA, Catholic Charities, Lutheran Social Services, the Salvation Army, the Urban League, and the United Way. They and a number of others and their local affiliates are strong, nationally established nonprofits that have contracts in two or more states. See

U.S. General Accounting Office (GAO), "Welfare Reform: Interim Report on the Potential Ways to Strengthen Federal Oversight of State and Local Contracting," GAO-02-245, April 2002, p. 14.

3. Paul Light, *Making Nonprofits Work* (Brookings, 2000).

4. Lester Salamon, *Partners in Public Service: Government-Nonprofit Relations in the Modern Welfare State* (Johns Hopkins University Press, 1995), p. 88.

5. Linda M. Lampkin and Thomas H. Pollack, *The New Nonprofit Almanac and Desk Reference: The Essential Facts and Figures for Managers, Researchers, and Volunteers* (Urban Institute, 2002), table 5.8.

6. Ibid., pp. 100–01.

7. Eric Twombly, "Human Services Nonprofits in Metropolitan Areas during Devolution and Welfare Reform" (Urban Institute, 2000).

8. Carol J. De Vita, "Nonprofits and Devolution: What Do We Know?" in Elizabeth T. Boris and C. Eugene Steuerle, eds., *Nonprofits and Government: Collaboration and Conflict* (Urban Institute, 1999), p. 221.

9. Twombly's research pointed to the greater ability that larger, older non-profits (providing core welfare-reform services) have to survive changes to the environment induced by welfare reform. In part this reflects the long-standing relationships of older nonprofits with funders and other groups that may have buffered their operations. See Eric Twombly, "Welfare Reform's Impact on the Failure Rate of Nonprofit Human Service Providers" (Urban Institute, 2000).

10. Twombly, "Human Services Nonprofits."

11. Lester Salamon, *Holding the Center: America's Nonprofit Sector at a Crossroads* (New York: Nathan Cummings Foundation, 1997), p. 41.

12. Ibid., pp. 41–42.

13. Jennifer R. Wolch, *The Shadow State: Government and Voluntary Sector in Transition* (New York: Foundation Center, 1990), p. 19.

14. Nancy Liu, executive director, Chinese Community Center, Houston; interview with Philippe Rosse, August 3, 2000.

15. Sister Raymonda DuVall, executive director, Catholic Charities, San Diego; interview with author, July 20, 2000.

16. From presentation at American Public Human Services Association Conference, "Boosting Effectiveness in Urban Welfare Programs," Washington, July 19, 2000.

17. Richard Shaw, chief executive officer, Community Services of the AFL-CIO, Houston, Texas; interview with Philippe Rosse, August 1, 2000.

18. Amalia V. Betanzos, president, Wildcat, Inc., New York City, and Jeffrey Jablow, executive vice president; interview with author, May 16, 2000.

19. Ibid.

20. Rex Davidson, chief executive officer, Goodwill Industries of New York; interview with author, June 7, 2000.

21. Goodwill won a $35.4 million Skills Assessment and Job Placement Center contract for the period October 1, 1999–September 30, 2002, and a $49.4 million Employment Services and Job Placement Center contract for December 1, 1999–November 30, 2002.

22. Goodwill currently has twelve subcontractors.

23. Nancy Biberman, "Recommendations for Structural and Policy Changes to Link Workforce Development and Economic Development: A Practitioner View from the South Bronx Field," Women's Housing and Economic Development Corporation, December 2001, p. 4.

24. Mike Johnson, "County Workers Get Key W-2 Role: $5 Million Contract to Provide for Initial Assessments of Clients," *Milwaukee Journal Sentinel,* September 19, 2001, p. 3B.

25. Milwaukee, like many sites in Wisconsin, Florida, and Arizona, provides for contractors to assume all aspects of TANF including eligibility determination, a function that most states still provide themselves. See Pamela Winston and others, "Privatization of Welfare Services: A Literature Review," Mathematica Policy Research, Inc., 8834-002, Washington, May 2002, p. 11.

26. De Vita and Twombly used 1992–94 Internal Revenue Service data to examine the number, types, and financial stability of human services organizations most likely to be affected by welfare reform. Of these, 83 percent offered core services. The study showed that these organizations faced financial uncertainty and increasingly stringent budgets. As a result only 41 percent reported positive net balance sheets for 1992 and 1994. See De Vita, "Nonprofits and Devolution."

27. William Grinker, president of Seedco/N-PAC; interview with author, May 18, 2000.

28. Tracie McMillan, "The Great Training Robbery," *City Limits,* May 2001.

29. Diane Baillargeon, senior vice president, Seedco, quoted in "New Solutions for Changing Times," Report of Seedco and its affiliate N-PAC, Partnerships for Community Development, July 1999, p. 16.

30. See Jessica Yates, "Case Studies on Non-Profits' Involvement in Contracting for Welfare Services," Welfare Information Network, September 9, 1997; author's interview with Rita Rinner, chief operating officer, YW-Works, April 23, 2001.

31. Rinner, interview with author, April 23, 2001.

32. Ibid.

33. Rachel Miller, vice president for operations and fiscal affairs and director of workforce development, Women's Housing and Economic Development Corporation (WHEDCO); interview with author, July 17, 2000.

34. Liu, interview with Philippe Rosse, Houston, August 3, 2000.

35. Diane Baillargeon, senior vice president of Seedco and chief operating officer of the Non-Profit Assistance Corporation, recently reported that they have a waiting list of nonprofits that want to work under their umbrella, but the size of their contracts limits the number they can work with. They are currently at capacity. *A View from the Frontlines: Innovations in the Delivery of Welfare Services,* Brookings Forum, Washington, October 17, 2001.

36. This model is the prevailing one under the U.S. Department of Labor's Work Force Investment Act, where eligible clients are provided with independent training accounts (ITAs) to use for training with qualified providers.

37. One anonymous reviewer pointed out, however, that reverse-referral contracts can be of significant benefit to a nonprofit if its primary raison d'être is pro-

viding another service where training and employment are part of a broader service mix and it can benefit considerably from the added resources that are provided by a reverse-referral contract's reimbursement for job placement.

38. Richard Shaw, chief executive officer of community services of the AFL-CIO, Houston, Texas; interview with Philippe Rosse, August 1, 2000.

39. U.S. GAO, "Welfare Reform," GAO-02-245, pp. 18–38.

40. Ibid.

41. Biberman, "Recommendations for Structural and Policy Changes."

42. Holly Payne, director of Welfare Services, MAXIMUS; interview with Paul Light, June 8, 2000.

43. Data provided by the New York City Comptroller's Office, Office of Contracts.

44. Anita Moses, president, Education and Planning Institute; interview with author, June 27, 2000.

45. Carol Anderson, executive director, Lockheed Martin IMS, Houston, Texas; interview with Philippe Rosse, August 5, 2000.

46. Jesse Castanada, president, SER-Jobs for Progress of Houston; interview with Philippe Rosse, Houston, Texas, August 4, 2000.

47. U.S. GAO, "Welfare Reform: Federal Oversight of State and Local Contracting," GAO-02-661, June 11, 2002, pp. 35–36.

48. Data provided by Swati Desai, acting executive deputy administrator for policy and programs, New York City Human Resources Administration.

49. GAO, "Welfare Reform," GAO-02-661, pp. 35–36. Performance was rarely associated strongly with for-profit status. Indeed, the for-profits were just as likely to fall short as the nonprofits.

50. Anita Moses, president, Education and Planning Institute; interview with author, June 27, 2000.

51. Richard Bonamarte, executive vice president, Wildcat Services Corporation; formerly executive deputy administrator for contracts and procurement, New York City Human Resources Administration; interview with author, January 25, 2002.

52. Biberman, "Recommendations for Structural and Policy Changes."

53. William P. Ryan, "The New Landscape for Nonprofits," *Harvard Business Review,* vol. 77, no. 1 (January/February 1999), pp. 127–36; Peter Frumkin and Alice Andre-Clark, "The Rise of the Corporate Social Worker," *Society,* vol. 36, no. 6 (September/October 1999), p. 46.

54. Baillargeon, *A View from the Frontlines.*

55. PA Summary Report provided by Swati Desai, acting executive deputy administrator for policy and programs, New York City Human Resources Administration; CalWORKS Welfare to Work Monthly Progress reports provided by Greg Baldwin, principal administrative analyst, Policy and Program Support Division, County of San Diego, Health and Human Services Agency.

Chapter 5

1. Data are from the 1992 U.S. Census of service industries and are reported

in Peter Frumkin and Alice Andre-Clark, "The Rise of the Corporate Social Worker," *Society,* vol. 36, no. 6 (September/October 1999), pp. 46–54.

2. Peter Frumkin and Alice Andre-Clark, "When Missions, Markets, and Politics Collide: Values and Strategy in the Non-Profit Human Services," *Non-Profit and Voluntary Sector Quarterly,* vol. 29, no. 1 (Supplement 2000), pp. 141–63. Frumkin and Andre-Clark rely on the U.S. Census Bureau, "Service Annual Survey: 1996" (Washington, 1998), for their estimates of growth and market share.

3. Frumkin and Andre-Clark, "When Missions, Markets, and Politics Collide."

4. IMS was recently sold by Lockheed Martin to Affiliated Computer Services (ACS). Because most of the contract activity analyzed here came before the merger, reference throughout will be to Lockheed Martin IMS.

5. In 1998, Benova, Inc., headquartered in Portland, Oregon, was acquired by AFSA Data Corporation, itself a wholly owned affiliate of FleetBoston Financial Corporation. Benova, Inc., acquired Curtis & Associates, headquartered in Kearney, Nebraska, in 2000. In 2002, Benova, Inc., Curtis & Associates, and the government contracting division of AFSA Data Corporation, headquartered in Long Beach, California, became the Concera Corporation. Concera specializes in contracting with federal, state, and local government agencies to provide a wide range of business process outsourcing solutions. Because most of the contract activity analyzed here came before the merger, reference throughout will be to Curtis & Associates.

6. Lee Bowes, CEO, America Works; interview with author, May 21, 2000.

7. Data on the national for-profits were collected through public documents for the public companies and through interviews with national executives. Not all were willing to share detailed data on their contracts, growth, and financial status that they felt to be proprietary. This resulted in data gaps and comparability issues. Comparable data were particularly difficult to obtain from ARBOR and America Works (see box 5-1).

8. Goodwill in Milwaukee bid for and won its initial contracts as a subsidiary known as Employment Solutions. In the current round of contracts, following a state audit that revealed inappropriate and questionable expenditures for Employment Solutions and others, Employment Solutions agreed to drop out of consideration, and its service region was distributed between two of the remaining contractors.

9. Dick Buschmann, administrator of the financial assistance division for the Milwaukee County Department of Human Services; interview with author, April 24, 2001.

10. Ruth Vaala-Strong, chief operating officer, Curtis & Associates, Inc.; interview with author, May 17, 2000.

11. Curtis & Associates website: www.selfsufficiency.com/index.html.

12. George Leutermann was formerly a Goodwill executive and administrator in child protection in Milwaukee; he later held a number of positions in the Wisconsin W-2 welfare reform effort. Some of his major accomplishments in these areas include large-scale outsourcing and privatization efforts.

13. George Leutermann, interview with author, January 13, 2000.

14. Jerry Stepaniak, current vice president, Welfare Reform Division, MAX-IMUS, and project director, Milwaukee; interview with author, April 25, 2001.

15. George Leutermann, interview with author, January 13, 2000.

16. Ibid.

17. Ibid.

18. David Heaney, project director, San Diego, MAXIMUS; interview with author, October 30, 2000.

19. Lee Bowes, CEO and cofounder of America Works; interview with author, May 24, 2000.

20. Peter Cove, founder of America Works, was quoted in a CNN interview in 1997 that America Works had experienced a 30 percent growth rate each year since 1984. See "Who's in Charge," August 21, 1997, transcript #97082102FN-L06.

21. Lee Bowes, interview with author, May 24, 2000.

22. One anonymous reviewer, critical of America Works's historical performance, noted that it was relatively unsuccessful as a nonprofit operator of a supported-work site in Boston and later performed poorly in Cleveland, the next major contract it won after incorporating as a for-profit.

23. www.maximus.com/public/virtual/investor/workforceservice.

24. Nancy Biberman, executive director, WHEDCO; interview with author, February 13, 2002.

25. Ibid.

26. Data provided by Swati Desai, acting executive deputy administrator, New York City Human Resources Administration (HRA), from the PA Summary Report as of October 15, 2001. Critics question the data, however, pointing to the vendor's ability to manipulate its reporting or otherwise exclude hard-to-place referrals that would reduce its performance.

27. Ed Gund, chief operating officer and senior vice president, Lockheed Martin IMS; interview with author and Paul Light, January 12, 2000.

28. Federal PRWORA legislation has created a five-year total lifetime cap on benefit receipt. Employed recipients whose jobs are partially financed through grant diversion run down the clock during this period of employment.

29. David Heaney, project director, San Diego, MAXIMUS; interview with author, October 30, 2000.

30. Ibid.

31. Katherine Barrett and Richard Greene, *Powering Up: How Public Managers Can Take Control of Information Technology* (CQ Press, 2000.)

32. Thomas Grissen, president, Government Operations Group, MAXIMUS; interview with Paul Light, June 8, 2000.

33. In eligibility determination, MAXIMUS has both the contract in Milwaukee County and a pilot project in Maricopa County, Arizona. Lockheed Martin IMS has a pilot program to determine eligibility in Florida and has benefit determination in most of its contracts in Florida and Texas. It is part of the one-stop blueprint that Lockheed is trying to achieve when it bids on both front-

end and direct-service contracts and is thus reflected in the large average size of its contracts. See appendix B.

34. The incentive payments notwithstanding, a recent impact study of Arizona Works revealed few significant differences between the performance of MAX-IMUS and that of Maricopa County. See Bob Kornfield, "Evaluation of the Arizona Works Pilot Program: Second Impact Study Report," Abt Associates, Cambridge, Mass., February 2002.

35. Thomas Grissen, interview with Paul Light, June 8, 2000.

36. David Heaney, interview with author, October 30, 2000.

37. David Mastran, CEO, MAXIMUS; interview with Paul Light, June 8, 2000.

38. Holly Payne, director of welfare services, MAXIMUS; interview with Paul Light, June 8, 2000.

39. David Mastran, interview with Paul Light, June 8, 2000.

40. Holly Payne, interview with Paul Light, June 8, 2000.

41. Average taken from information provided by Akbar Piloti, executive vice president, Welfare Reform Division, MAXIMUS.

42. Holly Payne, interview with Paul Light, June 8, 2000.

43. Comparison between figures provided by Tom Scott, Contracts/Compliance Manager, Lockheed Martin IMS.

44. Information provided by Tom Scott.

45. See appendix B for individual vendor contract descriptions and values.

46. Only eight states have 50 percent or more of their contracted funds with for-profits (Utah, Nevada, Nebraska Washington, D.C., New Mexico, Florida, Hawaii, and Wyoming), and only two of them (Hawaii and Wyoming) have 100 percent. Florida has 70 percent of its contracted funds with for-profit contractors, most with Lockheed Martin IMS.

47. Holli Ploog, president, DynCorp Management Resources, Inc.; interview with author, January 12, 2000.

48. In many areas, current contractors whose performance has been good have the possibility to renew current contracts. How many will change hands due to poor performance or contractors' preferences is an open question. New York City has recently indicated that performance may not be the only, or even the primary, criterion of renewal. Whether this reflects a discomfort with the data or other political considerations is unclear, but it clearly undermines a principal argument of those proposing the virtues of competition.

49. See appendix B for more information.

50. Gabriel Ross, president, Education and Training, ARBOR, Inc.; interview with author, October 19, 2000.

51. U.S. Securities and Exchange Commission, Form 10-K, for fiscal year ended September 30, 2001, DynCorp, p. 11.

52. Holli Ploog, interview with Paul Light and author, January 12, 2000.

53. U.S. Securities and Exchange Commission, Form 10-K, for fiscal year ended September 30, 2001, MAXIMUS, Inc., p. 12.

54. David Mastran, interview with Paul Light, June 8, 2000.

55. U.S. Securities and Exchange Commission, Form 10-K, for fiscal year ended September 30, 2001, MAXIMUS, Inc., p. 12.

56. David Mastran, interview with Paul Light, June 8, 2000.

57. Information published on Lockheed Martin website, www.lockheed-martin.com.

58. David Mastran, interview with author, June 8, 2000.

59. Jerry Stepaniak, current vice president, Welfare Reform Division, MAXIMUS, and project director, Milwaukee, speaking at Brookings Forum, "A View from the Frontlines: Innovation in the Delivery of Welfare Services," Washington, October 17, 2001.

60. See appendix A.

61. David Heaney, interview with author, October 30, 2000.

62. Holly Payne, director of Welfare Services, MAXIMUS; interview with Paul Light, June 8, 2000.

63. Jerry Stepaniak, interview with author, April 25, 2001.

64. David Mastran, interview with Paul Light, June 8, 2000.

65. U.S. General Accounting Office, "Welfare Reform: Federal Oversight of State and Local Contracting Can Be Strengthened," GAO-02-661, June 11, 2002.

Chapter 6

1. Lester Salamon recognized a decade ago that "third-party government" is an increasingly standard pattern of the federal government in the domestic sphere, which allows government to do what it does best—"raising resources and setting societal priorities through a democratic political process—while utilizing the private sector for what it does best—organizing production of goods and services. In the process it reconciles the traditional American hostility to government with the recent American fondness for the services that modern society has increasingly required government to provide." See Lester Salamon, ed., *Beyond Privatization: The Tools of Government Action* (Urban Institute, 1989), pp. 10–11.

2. Paul Light, *Tides of Reform* (Brookings, 2000).

3. Ibid.

4. Peter Frumkin and Alice Andre-Clark, "When Missions, Markets, and Politics Collide: Values and Strategy in the Non-Profit Human Services," *Non-Profit and Voluntary Sector Quarterly*, vol. 29, no. 1 (Supplement 2000), pp. 141–63.

5. Sister Raymonda DuVall, Catholic Charities, San Diego; interview with author, July 19, 2000.

6. William J. Grinker argues that there are no magic or big-bang solutions to the problem of getting welfare recipients into decent-paying jobs. Nevertheless, the community-based nonprofits need help with the bread-and-butter issues of running their organizations. See William J. Grinker, "Building a Workforce Development Structure in New York," keynote speech at the conference "Beyond JTPA and Welfare to Work: Building a Workforce Development Infrastructure," Tarrytown, N.Y., November 11, 1999.

7. Ibid.

8. Ibid., p. 5.

9. ARBOR and Curtis & Associates, in particular, noted that they do not generally pay more than their nonprofit counterparts.

10. Wildcat, Inc.

11. These findings support conclusions from Paul Light, *The New Public Service* (Brookings, 1999.)

12. Sally Hazzard, project director, Lockheed Martin IMS, San Diego; interview with author, October 30, 2000.

13. It may be that nonprofits have a comparative advantage in attracting mission-driven employees. In Paul Light's study, public policy graduates who gravitated toward the nonprofit sector were more satisfied than those who went to government and the private sector, but they were also more likely to find their jobs stressful. Over time they were more likely to leave.

14. I am grateful to an anonymous reviewer for suggesting this point.

15. Paul Light, *The New Public Service*. His work has reinforced classic studies on the declining attractiveness of public service such as Charles Levine and Rosslyn S. Kleeman, "The Quiet Crisis in American Public Service," in Patricia W. Ingraham and Donald F. Kettl, eds., *Agenda for Excellence: Public Service in America* (Chatham House, 1992). See also National Commission on the Public Service, *Leadership for America: Rebuilding the Public Service, Report of the National Commission on the Public Service* (Washington, 1989).

16. A recent survey of all states and the District of Columbia and the counties with the largest TANF-funded for-profit contracting revealed how limited performance- or incentive-based contracting remains. Although contracting is very widespread, performance- or incentive-based contracts represent only 20 percent of the mix, 59 percent were straight cost reimbursement, and 24 percent were fixed price. It is curious, given the potential benefits touted by proponents of paying for performance, that most contracting agencies have either limited capacity to develop such arrangements or reservations about the comparative advantages of doing so. See U.S. General Accounting Office (GAO), "Welfare Reform: Federal Oversight of State and Local Contracting Can Be Strengthened," GAO-02-661, June 11, 2002, p. 18.

17. In *Leadership Counts,* Robert Behn emphasizes the value of holding managers accountable for measurable outcomes rather than specifying the means they must use. Allowing looseness with respect to the means promotes innovation, while tightness of outcomes ensures accountability. See Robert Behn, *Leadership Counts* (Harvard University Press, 1992).

18. Rex Davidson, chief executive officer, Goodwill Industries of New York; interview with author, June 20, 2000.

19. See U.S. GAO, "Welfare Reform," GAO-02-661, p. 18.

20. Ibid., pp. 18–38.

21. Informal discussions with the executive deputy administrator of Reporting and Accountability at New York City's Human Resources Administration revealed that performance will not serve as the sole determinant of contract renewals, but final criteria are still under consideration.

22. Mark Hoover, first deputy commissioner of the New York City Human Resources Administration; interview with author, June 29, 2000.

23. James A. Krauskopf, "Privatization of Human Services in New York City: Some Examples and Lessons," paper presented at the Annual Research Conference of the Association for Public Policy Analysis and Management, October, 1995. Based on work supported by the Twentieth Century Fund.

Further Reading

Auger, Deborah, and Kathryn Denhardt. "Privatization and Contracting: Managing for State and Local Productivity." *Public Productivity and Management Review* 22, no. 4 (June 1999).

Barnow, Burt S., and John Trutko. "Analysis of Performance Based Contracting in Human Resource Administrative Programs in New York City." Draft paper prepared under contract to HRA, March 2002.

Barrett, Katherine, and Richard Greene. *Powering Up: How Public Managers Can Take Control of Information Technology*. CQ Press, 2000.

Behn, Robert D. *Leadership Counts*. Harvard University Press, 1991.

———. *Rethinking Democratic Accountability*. Brookings, 2001.

Behn, Robert D., and Peter Kant. "Strategies for Avoiding the Pitfalls of Performance Contracting." *Public Productivity and Management Review*. June 1999.

Berkowitz, Bill. "Prospecting among the Poor: Welfare Privatization." Applied Research Center, May 2001.

Bernstein, Nina. "Squabble Puts Welfare Deals under Spotlight in New York." *New York Times* (February 22, 2000): B1.

Bezdek, Barbara. "Contractual Welfare: Non-Accountability and Diminished Democracy in Local Government Contracts for Welfare-to-Work Services." *Fordham Urban Law Journal* 28 (June 2001): rev. 1559.

Biberman, Nancy. "Recommendations for Structural and Policy Changes to Link Workforce Development and Economic Development: A Practitioner View from the South Bronx Field." Women's Housing and Economic Development Corporation. December 2001.

Boris, Elizabeth T., and C. Eugene Steuerle, eds. *Nonprofits and Government Collaboration and Conflict*. Urban Institute Press, 1999.

Brodkin, Evelyn, Carolyn Fuqua, and Katarina Thoren. "A Map of the New World: The Changing Face of Welfare-to-Work Intermediaries." Working paper, Project on the Public Economy of Work, University of Chicago, November 2001.

Cohen, Steven, and William Eimicke. "Overcoming Operational Obstacles to Privatization: The Art and Craft of Contracting." Paper prepared for the 2001 Research Meeting of the Association of Policy Analysis and Management, Washington, November 1–3, 2001.

Cruthirds, C. T. "The Community Action Program Agency and Voluntary Delegate Organizations: Issues in Interorganizational Contracting." Ph.D. dissertation, Tulane University, 1972.

Curtis & Associates, Inc., website, http://selfsufficiency.com/index.html.

DeHoog, Ruth H. *Contracting Out for Human Services: Economic, Political, and Organizational Perspectives.* State University of New York Press, 1984.

De Vita, Carol. "Nonprofits and Devolution: What Do We Know?" In *Nonprofits and Government Collaboration and Conflict,* edited by Elizabeth T. Boris and C. Eugene Steuerle. Urban Institute Press, 1999.

Donahue, John D. *The Privatization Decision: Public Ends, Private Means.* Basic Books, 1989.

DynCorp website, www.dyncorp.com.

Eimicke, William B. "San Diego County's Innovation Program: Using Competition and a Whole Lot More to Improve Public Services." Grant Report, PricewaterhouseCoopers Endowment for the Business of Government, 2000.

Ewoh, Andrew. "An Inquiry into the Role of Public Employees and Managers in Privatization." *Review of Public Personnel Administration* 19, no. 1 (Winter 1999): 8–27.

Frumkin, Peter, and Alice Andre-Clark. "The Rise of the Corporate Social Worker." *Society* 36, no. 6 (September/October 1999).

————. "When Missions, Markets and Politics Collide: Values and Strategy in the Non-Profit Human Services." *Non-Profit and Voluntary Sector Quarterly* 29, no.1, supplement (2000): 141–63.

Gibelman, Margaret, and Harold W. Demone Jr. "The Evolving Contract State." In *Services for Sale: Purchasing Health and Human Services,* edited by Harold W. Demone Jr. and Margaret Gibelman. Rutgers University Press, 1989.

————. *The Privatization of Human Services.* Springer, 1998.

Greene, Lisa. "County Sued over Lockheed Contract." *St. Petersburg Times,* January 8, 2002; *Largo Times:* 1.

Hodgkinson, Virginia. "Assessing the Role of the Nonprofit Sector Following Welfare Reform: What Do We Know? What Do We Need to Know?" Working Paper, Georgetown Public Policy Institute, Washington, 2000.

Ihrke, Douglas M. "Alternative Service Delivery in Milwaukee County: The Privatization of Welfare." Brookings Institution Center for Public Management, 2000.

Ingraham, Patricia, and Donald F. Kettl, eds. *Agenda for Excellence: Public Service in America.* Chatham House, 1992.

Johnson, Jocelyn M., and Barbara S. Romzek. "Contracting and Accountability in State Medicaid Reform: Rhetoric, Theories, and Reality." *Public Administration Review* 59, no. 5 (1999): 383–99.

Johnson, Michael. "County Workers Get Key W-2 Role: $5 Million Contract to Provide for Initial Assessments of Clients." *Milwaukee Journal Sentinel*, September 19, 2001: 3B.

Kamerman, Sheila B., and Alfred J. Kahn. *Privatization and the Welfare State.* Princeton University Press, 1989.

———. "Privatization, Contracting, and Reform of Child and Family Social Services." Washington: The Finance Project, 1998.

Kettl, Donald F. *Sharing Power: Public Governance and Private Markets.* Brookings, 1993.

———. *The Global Public Management Revolution: A Report on the Transformation of Governance.* Brookings, 2000.

Kohut, Andrew. *Deconstructing Distrust: How Americans View Government.* The Pew Research Center, March 1998.

Kornfeld, Robert. *Evaluation of the Arizona Works Pilot Program: Second Impact Study Report.* Cambridge, Mass., Abt Associates, February 2002.

Kramer, R. M. "An Analysis of Policy Issues in Relationships between Government and Voluntary Social Welfare Agencies." Ph.D. dissertation, University of California, Berkeley, 1964.

Krauskopf, James A. "Privatization of Human Services in New York City: Some Examples and Lessons." Paper presented at the Annual Research Conference of the Association for Public Policy Analysis and Management, October 1995.

———. "What Matters in Managing and Assessing Public Human Services?" November 5, 1997.

———. "Government Contracting and Direct Operations: Issues and Opportunities in Human Service Programs." Paper presented at the Annual Research Conference of the Association for Public Policy Analysis and Management, October 1998.

———. "Reforming the Public Child Welfare System in New York." Corporation for Supportive Housing, November 4, 1999.

Lampkin, Linda, and Thomas H. Pollack. *The New Nonprofit Almanac and Desk Reference: The Essential Facts and Figures for Managers, Researchers and Volunteers.* Urban Institute, 2002.

Levin, Martin A., and Mary Bryna Sanger. *Making Government Work.* Jossey-Bass, 1994.

Light, Paul. *The New Public Service.* Brookings, 1999.

———. *Making Nonprofits Work: A Report on the Tides of Nonprofit Management Reform.* Brookings, 2000.

———. *Tides of Reform.* Brookings, 2000.

Lipton, Eric. "Hevesi Quietly Drops 10-Month Fight to Block Welfare-to-Work Contracts." *New York Times*, December 2, 2000.

Lockheed Martin Annual Report, www.lockheedmartin.com/investor/annualreport/1999annualreport.pdf.

MAXIMUS 1999 Annual Report, www.maximus.com/pdf/AnnualReport.pdf.

McMillan, Tracie. "The Great Training Robbery." *City Limits,* May 2001.

Milward, H. Brinton. "Implications of Contracting Out: New Roles for the Hollow State." In *New Paradigms for Government: Issues for the Changing Public Service,* edited by Patricia Ingraham and others, 41–62. Jossey-Bass, 1994.

Minogue, Martin, and others, eds. *Beyond the New Public Management: Changing Ideas and Practices in Governance.* Edward Elgar, 1998.

Moe, Ronald C. "Managing Privatization: A New Challenge to Public Administration." In *Agenda for Excellence 2: Administering the State,* edited by Guy B. Peters and Bert A. Rockman. Chatham House, 1996.

National Commission on the Public Service. *Leadership for America: Rebuilding the Public Service, Report of the National Commission on the Public Service.* Washington, 1989.

Olson, Mancur. *The Logic of Collective Action.* Harvard University Press, 1965.

Osborne, David E., and Ted Gaebler. *Reinventing Government: How the Entrepreneurial Spirit Is Transforming the Public Sector.* Plume, 1993.

Prager, Jonas, and Swati Desai. "Privatizing Local Government Operations." *Public Productivity & Management Review* 20, no. 2 (1996): 185–203.

Riccardi, Nicholas. "County Nears Private Bids on Welfare Reform." *Los Angeles Times,* February 8, 2000, B1.

Rom, Mark Carl. "From Welfare to States Opportunity, Inc.: Public-Private Partnerships in Welfare Reform." *American Behavioral Scientist* (September 1999).

Romzek, Barbara S., and Jocelyn M. Johnson. "Reforming Medicaid through Contracting: The Nexus of Implementation and Organizational Culture." *Journal of Public Administration Theory and Research* 9, no. 1 (1999): 107–39.

Roper, Richard W. "A Shifting Landscape: Contracting for Welfare Services in New Jersey." *Rockefeller Reports.* Nelson A. Rockefeller Institute of Government, 1998.

Ryan, W. P. "Background, Research and Opinion: For Profit Human Service Providers." Pew Charitable Trusts, 1997.

———. "The New Landscape for Nonprofits." *Harvard Business Review* 77, no. 1 (January/February 1999).

Salamon, Lester M. "Rethinking Public Management: Third Party Government and the Changing Forms of Government Action." *Public Policy* 29, no. 3 (Summer 1981).

———. *Partners in Public Service: Government-Nonprofit Relations in the Modern Welfare State.* Johns Hopkins University Press, 1995.

———. *Holding the Center: America's Nonprofit Sector at a Crossroads.* Nathan Cummings Foundation, 1997.

Salamon, Lester M., ed. *Beyond Privatization: The Tools of Government Action.* Urban Institute Press, 1989.

Savas, E. S. *Privatization: The Key to Better Government.* Chatham House, 1987.

———. *Privatization and Public-Private Partnerships.* Chatham House, 2000.

Savas, E. S., Paul Andrisani, and Simon Hakim. "The New Public Management: Lessons from Innovating Governors and Mayors." Baruch College, City University of New York, Center for Competitive Government. February 15, 2002.

Sclar, Elliott D. *You Don't Always Get What You Pay For: The Economics of Privatization.* Cornell University Press, 2000.

Smith Nightingale, Demetra, and Nancy Pindus. "Privatization of Public Social Services: A Background Paper." Urban Institute, October 15, 1997.

Smith, Steven Rathgeb, and Michael Lipsky. *Non-Profits for Hire: The Welfare State in the Age of Contracting.* Harvard University Press, 1993.

Twombly, Eric. "Human Services Nonprofits in Metropolitan Areas during Devolution and Welfare Reform." Urban Institute, 2000.

———. "Welfare Reform's Impact on the Failure Rate of Nonprofit Human Service Providers." Urban Institute, 2000.

U.S. Bureau of the Census. "Service Annual Survey: 1996." Washington, 1998.

U.S. General Accounting Office. "Privatization: Lessons Learned by State and Local Governments." GAO/GGD-97-48. Report to the chairman, House Republican Task Force on Privatization. March 1997.

———. "Social Service Privatization: Expansion Poses Challenges in Ensuring Accountability for Program Results." GAO/HEHS-98-6. Report to the chairman, Subcommittee on Human Resources, Committee on Government Reform and Oversight, House of Representatives. October 1997.

———. "Welfare Reform: Interim Report on Potential Ways to Strengthen Federal Oversight of State and Local Contracting." GAO-02-245. April 2002.

———. "Welfare Reform: Federal Oversight of State and Local Contracting Can Be Strengthened." GAO-02-661. June 2002.

Warner, Mildred E., and Robert Hebdon. "Local Government Restructuring: Privatization and Its Alternatives." *Journal of Policy Analysis and Management* 20, no. 2 (Spring 2001).

Warner, Mildred, and Amir Hefetz. "Privatization and the Market Restructuring Role of Local Government." Paper presented at the Economic Policy Institute Conference on Privatization, Washington, January 11, 2000.

Weaver, Kent. *Ending Welfare as We Know It.* Brookings, 2000.

Wendel, K. R. "Government Contracting for Purchase of Service." *Social Work* 21 (1976).

Wolch, Jennifer. *The Shadow State: Government and Voluntary Sector in Transition.* Foundation Center, 1990.

Wolf, Richard. "Public Aid Going Private in Many States." *USA Today,* August 3, 1998.

Yates, Jessica. "Case Studies on Non-Profits' Involvement in Contracting for Welfare Services." Welfare Information Network, 1997. www.financeproject-info.org/WIN.

Index

2, 11, 17; federal funding, 2, 13;
NYC, 36–38; private sector and,
13–16; public officials and,
36–39; reforms, 2–3, 12–16, 20,
28–30, 36–39, 94–97; services,
4–7; term limits, 34; voluntary
organizations, 13; welfare-to-
work, 1, 19–23, 26–29, 37, 72,
89. *See also* Service delivery systems; *and specific legislation and
programs*
WEP, 56
WHEDCO. *See* Women's Housing
and Economic Development Corporation
Wildcat Service Corporation, 23, 53,
56, 71, 82, 84
Wisconsin, 34; state legislature, 43,
56–57; Waukesha, 77. *See also*
Milwaukee

Wisconsin Works (W-2), 32
Women's Housing and Economic
Development Corporation
(WHEDCO), 56, 63–64, 83–84
Workers, 88–89
Workforce Investment Act (WIA) of
1998, 28, 64, 93–94; caseloads
and, 35; DOL and, 28–29, 64;
employment, 28–29; governments
and, 28–29; ITA, 29; one-stop
centers, 29, 94; programs, 65, 67

YMCA (Young Men's Christian
Association), 32, 100
YWCA (Young Women's Christian
Association), 60
YW-WORKS, 60, 84

Zinser, Joan, 35, 45